California AVOCADOS

A Delicious History

ROB CRISELL

AMERICAN PALATE

Published by American Palate
A Division of The History Press
Charleston, SC
www.historypress.com

For

My parents, Bob and Toni Crisell,

and

My wife, Monisha.

These trees he plants, and in whose shade he shall never sit, he loves for themselves, and for his children, and for his children's children, over whom their branches will extend.

—Hyacinthe Loyson, 1866

CONTENTS

ACKNOWLEDGMENTS

Those who sowed the first seeds of the state's avocado industry in 1915 and those who help it bear fruit today share a common passion for avocados that links them across time and space. *Industry* is an insufficient word for what has truly been a century-long love affair.

I am tremendously grateful to the many people who have helped make this book a reality. Through dozens of interviews and hundreds of hours spent in libraries and exploring online archives, I have developed a profound appreciation for what the citizens of Avocado Land have accomplished. For the past year, I have spoken with more than thirty-five growers, nurserymen, researchers, handlers, grove managers and dedicated amateurs. I am especially thankful to Bob Vice, Bob Lucy, Mike Sanders, Rob Brokaw and Charley Wolk for their early support.

I am deeply indebted to the members, past and present, of the California Avocado Society. The Society's annual yearbooks were an indispensable resource for me, as they have been for avocado researchers for more than a century. Thanks also to current Society directors, especially Greg Alder, Gary Bender, Wayne Brydon, Ben Faber and Carl Stucky.

I am grateful for the support of the California Avocado Commission, including Ken Melban, Terry Splane and Marji Morrow; the Hass Avocado Board, including Emiliano Escobedo and Nikki Ford; Calavo Growers (especially Lindsay Martinez) for sharing archival material on the exchange's storied history; and Phil Henry of Henry Avocados for reviewing chapter excerpts.

I have done my best to seek out the industry's leaders and catalysts, although I know that I was able to speak only to a small fraction of them. Thanks to all who interviewed with me (usually in person and at length), including Greg Alder, Mary Lu Arpaia, Scott Bauwens, Steve Barnard, Gary Bender, Rob Brokaw, Lee Cole, Sharon Colona and Scott Wibbenmeyer, Jan DeLyser, Emiliano Escobedo, Ben Faber, Eric Focht, Ralph Foster, Victor Gonzalez, Julie Frink, Robert Jackson, Bob Lucy, Steve Maddock, Gray Martin, Mike Sanders, Jaime Serrato, Corrine and Cid da Silva, Rick Shade, Al Stehly, Jerome Stehly, Scott Van Der Kar, Bob Vice, Steve Taft, Damien Vasquez, Rob Wedin, Charley Wolk and others.

I am also grateful to Kathy Musial of the Huntington Library and Botanical Gardens for access to the Shepherd-Brokaw Collection, which was lovingly curated and donated by Jack Shepherd and Carl Stucky on behalf of the Society. Thanks also to Raquel Folgado for guiding me through Huntington's historic avocado groves; Tom Frew of the Fallbrook Historical Society; the librarians at UC–Riverside Library for their help with the William T. Horne Memorial Avocado Collection; the reference staff of the Temecula Public Library; and Lila Hargrove of the Fallbrook Chamber of Commerce.

Thank you to Toni Crisell, Greg Alder, Bob Lucy and others who provided feedback on early drafts, as well as my acquisitions editor Laurie Krill at Arcadia Publishing for her patient guidance. Finally, I'd like to express my gratitude and love for my wife, Monisha, without whom this book—and this happy life—would not exist.

INTRODUCTION

An unripe avocado is of small charm to the palate, but a ripe one lives long in the memory of delicious flavors.
—from the first meeting of the California Avocado Association, 1915

Like the eternal snows of Wales for Dylan Thomas, the avocado groves of my youth seem more magical in my memory than when I first encountered them in the 1980s.

I grew up in the heart of a three-acre Fuerte grove in Fallbrook, California, a town in northern San Diego County nicknamed the "Avocado Capital of the World." In 1982, my parents came to Fallbrook from Orange County, their three children crammed into the back seat of a blue Dodge van. Like thousands of others fleeing the coastal cities, they sought a slower, more agricultural lifestyle for themselves and their offspring.

They built a house on a hill overlooking avocado groves that stretched for miles in all directions. For years, my sister and I would walk through those groves to our bus stop, wading through thick leaf mulch that crackled noisily in our wake. The old trees towered over us, their thick branches reaching up from the ground like gnarled gray hands, blotting out the sun to form dusky sanctuaries. Occasionally, the crash of a fat avocado onto the dry mulch bed would jolt us from our morning reveries.

For my siblings and me, avocados were the constant companions of an idyllic childhood. I remember avocado-throwing contests with friends, avocado festivals, ancient packinghouses and migrant workers thrusting

Fuerte avocado groves at the Crisell house in Fallbrook, circa 1981. *Author's collection.*

picking poles into canopies. As a teenager, I would sell fruit out of my car in the nearby desert communities. Our two grandfathers worked together to build a treehouse overlooking the chicken run. One year, our Labrador retriever consumed so many fallen avocados that we sent her to live with friends before she ate herself to death.

My parents' timing as hobbyist farmers was unfortunate. Between 1976 and 1987, avocado plantings in the state rose from twenty-four thousand acres to seventy-six thousand, most of which were located not far from our house. This boom led to a massive crop in 1987—and a historic bust in prices. Subsequent years would bring droughts, disease, development and rising water costs. After regrafting our trees to a new variety called Hass, my parents decided that they had had enough. In 1999, I was working on the East Coast when they called to tell me that they had sold the house.

A single thread of passion and perseverance connects the men and women of California who have spent their lives growing, selling and studying the avocado. The industry has survived more than a century of the slings and arrows of outrageous fortune. Through it all, growers, packers, nurserymen, pickers, retailers, marketers and researchers continue to devote themselves to a fruit that gives the world so much joy.

The groves around my childhood home are mostly gone now, as are many of the legendary plantings around Fallbrook. Total acreage in the state is half what it was in the 1980s. But this book is not the history of a once-great industry fading into irrelevance. Far from it. In the words of Alfred Lord Tennyson, "though much is taken, much abides." California is and always will be Avocado Land.

So, whether you are enjoying avocado toast in Sydney, a rainbow roll in Vancouver or an avocado coffee-shake in Jakarta, you can thank the Golden State and its growers for their part in introducing this delightful fruit to the world.

AVOCADOS BEFORE CALIFORNIA

PREHISTORY-1800

The Aguacat no less is Venus Friend
(To th'Indies Venus Conquest does extend)
A fragrant Leaf the Aguacata bears,
Her Fruit in fashion of an Egg appears.
—Abraham Cowley, 1661

Cast your memory back to the first time you tasted an avocado. More than likely, it was in the form of guacamole, or maybe it was it tucked inside a sandwich or a sushi roll. Do you remember whether you enjoyed it right away? Or did its subtle, nutty taste and buttery texture—so unlike an orange, peach or other more commonplace fruits—take time for you to appreciate? Regardless of those initial memories, if you are reading this book, you are likely among the billions of people who now adore this delicious green fruit. Perhaps you even agree with the lofty claim of Wilson Popenoe—one of California's early avocado pioneers—that the avocado is "God's greatest gift to humanity."

Most people raised in California during the 1980s ate avocados early and often. Californians fell in love with the fruit well before the rest of the world had ever laid eyes on one—or at least the world outside of Latin America. For Californians, the avocado is as much a part of the state as fine wine or surfing. True, these things did not originate here, but it often seems like it. In fact, the citizens of the Golden State can make a better claim for having "invented" the avocado than anyone else.

But before telling that story, let's begin with the basics.

WHAT IS AN AVOCADO?

The avocado is a member of the plant family known as Lauraceae, which takes its name from its most prominent member, the Grecian laurel tree (*Laurus nobilis*). Lauraceae are plants that have oil cells in the leaves, wood or fruit. Like avocados, most laurels are semi- or subtropical in origin. The leaves or bark of these trees are often aromatic when crushed, providing spices and flavoring. Famous examples include California bay, myrtle, sassafras, camphor and cinnamon. Certain subspecies of avocados have leaves that release an anise aroma when crushed, and the people of Latin America have used them in cooking and tea for millennia.

Within the Lauraceae family, the most famous genus might be the *Persea americana*—the avocado tree. Like other well-known plants from Latin America—corn, cacao, coffee, squash, vanilla, tomatoes, strawberries, potatoes and many others—the avocado is a "cultigen." A cultigen is a cultivated species that has gone through such extreme transformation under prehistoric human selection that its exact ancestry is now unknown. It is an evergreen tree, typically reaching average heights of between fifteen and thirty feet (although there have been trees more than one hundred feet high) and a spread of roughly the same, depending on the varietal and other factors. Avocado trees require temperate climates and more than an average amount of clean water and can live for more than a century.

Many early commentators compared the avocado to a pear, presumably because of the ovoid shape of most varieties. Botanically, however, avocados are very different from pears. The pear hails from the Rosaceae family and is a sweet and juicy pomaceous fruit like the apple. The high-fat, savory avocado, however, is actually a berry containing a single large seed.

While the avocado may be a cultigen, some researchers still call the fruit a "semi-domesticate" because it is strongly heterozygous, meaning that each tree inherits different alleles of a genomic marker from each biological parent. Due to this nature, every avocado seed represents a potentially new variety of avocado. It might be similar to its parents, but it might be quite different. Some might produce fruit and show a marked improvement over their parent tree, while most will be barren or possess inferior qualities. Today, there are an estimated nine hundred different known avocado varieties.

The only way to ensure a duplicate of the original avocado tree is to graft "scions" (usually the stem, shoot or bud) from that tree onto existing rootstock. While grafting is a practice going back thousands of years, it was not known in the New World until the mid-1800s. Until humans understood the science of grafting, cultivating avocado trees was always a gamble.

Humans have long been aware of striking differences between various types of avocados. In their reports on local flora, Spanish explorers took note of them. In the early decades of the twentieth century, "fruit explorers" such as Wilson Popenoe and David Fairchild began to systematically identify these differences in their trips to Mexico and Central America. It was not until the 1970s, however, that American scientists identified three subspecies or "races" within *Persea americana*: Mexican, Guatemalan and West Indian. The former two races originated in their eponymous countries, playing an important role among the megafauna of the Pleistocene. The West Indian race likely originated along the Pacific Coast of Central America and may have been the result of early attempts at domestication by Mesoamericans.

It is helpful to understand these underlying avocado types, since most avocados today are hybrids invented by enterprising California "nurserymen" in the first half of the twentieth century.

Mexican Race

Avocados in the Mexican race are fast-maturing and semitropical, which means that they can grow in colder soils and have more cold tolerance in general. This allows them to flourish at altitudes of five thousand to nine thousand feet in warmer climates. Unlike Guatemalans, they usually have thin green skins. The Mexican type was important for the development of rootstocks in California thanks to their large seeds and tendency to ripen quickly. Unlike Guatemalan and West Indian fruit, Mexican varietals have aromatic leaves, which are still used in Mexican cuisine and herbal teas. They are considered to be an excellent eating fruit, with the highest oil content of the three types.

No pure Mexican varieties are now available commercially in California. However, Mexican genes in hybrid cultivars such as Hass and Fuerte have played important roles in the state. GEM, one of the newer Hass-like hybrids, is rising in popularity, although Hass remains the world's dominant variety. The Mexican race lends its cold hardiness to the Guatemalan hybrids, as well as a faster growing capability. Varieties such as Mexicola, Duke and Topa Topa were popular in the early years of California's avocado industry.

Guatemalan Race

The Guatemalan race of avocados is subtropical, meaning that it has less cold tolerance than the Mexican race, reflective of its ancestral home in the highlands of Central America. Guatemalan avocados thrive at elevations of three thousand to six thousand feet in warm climates. Because they have a reputation for having a better flavor than those of either Mexican or West Indian, they were popular in California before hybrids took over. Guatemalan cultivars such as Nabal, Reed, Dickinson and Queen were considered some of the best eating fruit and can still be found in farmers' markets and among hobbyist or "backyard" growers. In addition to fruit quality, another salient characteristic is the length of time before fruit becomes mature. Guatemalan cultivars can require fifteen months from bloom to maturity.

Importantly, unlike the thin-skinned Mexican varietals, Guatemalan cultivars have thicker, harder skins that can make it difficult to tell when the fruit is ripe. One advantage of the thicker skin is that the fruit is less vulnerable to bruising during shipment.

West Indian Race

The third subspecies is the West Indian, which are natives of the tropical lowlands of Central America. West Indians were almost certainly the first types of avocados planted in the United States, in Florida in the early 1800s. Fruit size can often be very large, the skin is green and of medium thickness and they are fast-maturing like the Mexican. Since cold tolerance is the least among the three races, West Indian avocados such as Trapp, Waldin and Booth don't generally exist outside Florida and the Caribbean islands, although Africa and Asia also grow them. Because of their low oil content and sweeter flavor, most consider this subspecies to be inferior in terms of eating quality. On the other hand, they are more tolerant to saline water, which has led some researchers to experiment with West Indian rootstocks.

A "tropical" or West Indian avocado (*right*) shown next to a Hass. West Indian–type avocados can be three or four times larger than Mexican and Guatemalan hybrids, with much lower oil content. *Photo by Rob Crisell.*

18

Mexican-Guatemalan Hybrids

Since the beginning of California's avocado industry, most commercial cultivars have been Mexican-Guatemalan hybrids developed from chance seedlings. Predominantly Mexican cultivars include Bacon, Zutano, Shepard and Rincon, while predominantly Guatemalan crosses include Hass, Lamb, Gwen, Pinkerton and GEM.

PREHISTORIC AVOCADOS

Ethnobotanists speculate that wild avocados may have existed throughout North America as far back as 50 million years ago, co-evolving with the large mammals of the late Pleistocene epoch in Mexico and Central America. At that time, "megafauna"—mammals such as grizzly bear–sized ground sloths, mastodons, horses and other large species—roamed the continent. During the Pleistocene era, the large-seeded avocado evolved to attract these large animals that would eat it whole and then defecate it elsewhere, leading to widespread seed dispersal. Ethnobotanist Gary Nabhan speculates that megafauna would have selected fruit in much the same way humans do, by paying attention to ripeness, quality, flavor and oil content.

This mutualistic relationship ended abruptly as megafauna began to die out in a mass extinction around thirteen thousand years ago. Researchers believe that North America lost around 70 percent of its megafauna at this time, while South America lost upward of 80 percent. Whether as a result of catastrophic climate change or of overhunting by the newly arrived humans, or both, no one knows. However, the avocado, along with fruits like cherimoya and papaya, seemed doomed with the disappearance of their primary source of seed dispersal.

Luckily, giant sloths and other megafauna weren't the only ones who loved avocados. Some newcomers from the *Homo sapiens* species thought they were pretty tasty too.

EARLY MESOAMERICANS AND THE AHUÁCATL

The early settlement of the Americas is still the subject of ongoing study and debate. As archaeologists find new evidence of ever more ancient human occupations, they continue to adjust the arrival dates of the first

A Mayan woman holding a Guatemalan-type avocado, early 1900s. Botanist and industry founder Ira Condit wrote on the back of the photo, "Each fruit contains as much nourishment as a loaf of bread." *Courtesy of Shepherd-Brokaw Collection at the Huntington Library (SBC/THL).*

humans to North and South America. Whatever the timeframe may be, humans likely arrived in Mesoamerica just before or shortly after the extinction of the megafauna.

Mesoamericans have an ancient and storied relationship with trees, including the ceiba, rubber (zapote), chechen, cocoa and avocado. One of the central mythological traditions of many of the prehistoric peoples of the Americas incorporates "world trees" into art and religious traditions. A common belief was that gods and other spirits inhabited the forests, and humans had an obligation to safeguard these forests as a result. Archaeologists think that early hunter-gatherers would have valued the avocado as especially nutritious, working to curate natural stands of trees.

According to ethnobotanist Maria Elena Galindo-Tovar, avocado seed remains found in the Tehuacan Valley in the modern state of Puebla suggest that ancient peoples could have used avocados as early as 8000 BC and domesticated them since at least 5000 BC. When climatic conditions changed during Paleocene glaciations, avocados gradually moved south to Mesoamerica and its warmer climes. Gallindo-Tovar and her coauthors examined ethnohistoric and linguistic data, as well as archaeobotanical remains, to look for early utilization.

The Supe Valley in Peru was home to the Caral civilization, the oldest known culture in the Americas. Evidence for settlement here dates from 3100 BC, with avocado botanical remains suggesting that the tree has existed there since at least 1200 BC. This predates the use of maize or other grains. Evidence indicates that the avocado was integral in the diets of the people of the Moche Valley in northern Peru, whose civilization dates from 2500 to 1800 BC.

Another early culture in Mesoamerica was the Mokaya, who lived in southern Mexico and northern Guatemala between 1500 BC and 300 AD. While the Mokaya were known for their early cultivation of corn and cocoa, researchers think that they were also among the first to exploit the use of avocados as a food source, passing along their knowledge to the later Olmec and Mayan cultures.

The Mayans were among several Mesoamerican cultures to domesticate the avocado. Gallindo-Tovar thinks that iconographic data among surviving Mayan documents and tomb inscriptions show a close relationship between that culture and the avocado. For example, the fourteenth month of the Mayan calendar (developed between 800 BC and 300 BC) is represented by a glyph resembling the avocado. A tomb at the Mayan site of Palenque in Chiapas, Mexico, includes a carving of a tree with various fruits, including

THE HERMAPHRODITIC AVOCADO TREE

The avocado flower has both functional male and female organs. Trees flower in a manner known as "synchronous dichogamy." The male floral organ, which produces pollen, has both anthers and stamens. The female floral organ consists of the stigma (which receives the pollen), style and the ovary. During the pollination phase, flowers will open for only two days. When the flower first opens, it is in the female phase, and the stigma is receptive to pollen. The flower closes at the end of the female phase, which lasts a few hours. On the second day, the same flower reopens in the male phase and releases its pollen. This is the first step in avocado production, which results in fertilization and fruit set.

The timing of the male and female phases differs among varieties. There are two flowering types, referred to as "A" and "B" flower types. "A" varieties open as female on the morning of the first day. The flower closes in late morning or early afternoon. The flower stays closed until the afternoon of the second day, when it opens as male. "B" varieties open as female on the afternoon of the first day, close in late afternoon and reopen in the male phase the next morning. To encourage cross-pollination, growers will often plant a small number of "B" type trees (such as Zutano or Bacon) with their Hass trees, which are "A" types. Most varieties of avocados trees can self-pollinate, but studies have found that having "A" and "B" types together increases production by as much as 50 percent. In larger commercial groves, growers hand pollinate, use honey bee hives or even drones to help the pollination process.

Weather plays an important role in pollination. Temperatures must be suitable if flowers are to be fertilized properly. Extremely cold temperatures affect the number of pollinators (bees, wasps, ants, flies and others) that will visit the flowers and carry pollen from male to female. Intense winds and rains also negatively affect fertilization. Fruit development takes anywhere from five to fifteen months, depending on the variety.

the avocado. A city-state called Pusilha in what is now Belize is spelled using a glyph for the avocado, making it the "Kingdom of the Avocado."

Although archaeologists in Peru have found avocado seeds buried with Incan mummies dating back to 750 BC, the Incans probably did not begin cultivating avocados until the mid-1400s. In 1605, one of Pizarro's soldiers related that an Incan king had conquered a city called Palta around 1450 and brought back avocados he found there to Cuzco. Today, Peruvians and others still refer to the avocado as *palta*.

When the Spanish arrived in 1520, the Aztec civilization was the dominant culture in Mexico. The image of the avocado appears frequently in Aztec glyphs. The city of Ahuacatlan means "the place where the avocado abounds." In 1915, the glyph of an avocado tree with teeth became the logo of the California Avocado Association (later renamed the California Avocado Society), the world's oldest organization for the study and cultivation of the avocado.

An early report by Fray Toribio de Benavente (also known as Motolinía)—a Franciscan priest sent to New Spain soon after the conquest—the Aztec word for avocado was *ahuácatl*. From that word, the Spanish derived their name for the fruit—*aguacate* or *ahuacate*. One of the compound words in Aztec using *ahuácatl* is *āhuacamōlli*, which was a sauce or mixture (mole) using avocados. The Spanish, who soon came to adore this particular dish, renamed it guacamole.

While the media delights in repeating the salacious claim that *ahuácatl* derives from the Nahuatl word for "testicle," modern linguists have debunked this myth. At best, it seems Aztecs may have used *ahuácatl* as a euphemism for male gonads, the way English-speaking people employ the term "nuts." Still, avocados seemed to have had a reputation among Native peoples as an aphrodisiac. Allegedly, the Aztecs kept young women inside during the avocado harvest to discourage sexual assaults.

Spanish Contact and Colonial Times

The early Spanish conquistadores were notoriously rapacious in their lust for the gold and silver of the civilizations they conquered, especially those of the Aztec and Incan empires. As valuable as the precious metals were to the invaders, however, they ultimately paled in comparison to the value represented by the flora and fauna of the Americas. The many new species of fruits, nuts, vegetables, trees and other native plants brought back to Europe transformed the world. A partial list of these treasures includes tomatoes, corn, potatoes, pineapple, chili peppers, pumpkins, cocoa beans, papayas, tobacco, natural rubber and, yes, the avocado.

Martin Fernandez de Enciso, an attorney and cartographer on one of the earliest expeditions to the New World, wrote the first known description of the avocado. In his *Suma de Geografía*, published in Sevilla in 1519, Enciso described the fruit he saw in Yaharo (now Colombia) as "an orange, and when it is ready for eating it turns yellowish; that which it contains is like butter and is of marvelous flavor, so good and pleasing to the palate that it is a marvelous thing."

Fernandez de Oviedo—the official chronicler of the Spanish conquest, who accompanied Hernán Cortés in the early 1500s—gave a much more detailed description of the avocados he observed in northern South America and later in Nicaragua. In his *Summary of the Natural History of the Indias*, he wrote:

> On the mainland are certain trees that are called pear trees (perales). They are not pear trees like those of Spain, but are held in no less esteem; rather does this fruit have many advantages over the pears of that country. These are certain large trees, with long narrow leaves similar to the laurel, but larger and greener. This tree produces certain pears, many of which weigh more than a pound, and some less…and the color and shape is that of true pears, and the skin is somewhat thicker, but softer, and in the middle it holds a seed like a peeled chestnut…and between it and the primary skin is that which is eaten, which is something of a liquid or paste that is very similar to butter and a very good food and of good flavor.…[T]hey are wild trees.…for the chief gardener is God, and the Indians apply no work whatever.

Amusingly, Oviedo wrote that "after [avocados] are collected, they mature and become in perfect condition to be eaten; but…they spoil if they are left and allowed to pass that time." His observation about the famously short half-life of a ripe avocado is as true today as it was five hundred years ago.

Throughout the 1500s, dozens of other Spaniards mention the fruit in their writings. In 1594, Cervantes de Salazar observed that the avocado is similar to a fig but bigger. Garcilazo de la Vega in 1605 described it as a delicious and healthy fruit for sick people. Friar Francisco Ximénez mentions that Natives commonly used dried avocado leaves as toilet paper. In the mid-sixteenth century, Friar Diego Durán reported that people who lived in lands governed by the Aztecs gave them avocados in tribute. The Spanish also documented that the Aztecs sold avocados and other produce in the open-air markets of Tenochtitlan.

The Spanish chroniclers were also the first to remark on the diversity of avocados, including the three races later described by twentieth-century scientists in California. In his *History of the Indians of New Spain* in 1537, Fray

Fray Toribio de Benavente was one of the first Europeans to write about the *aguacate* and its importance in the New World. *Public domain.*

Benavente noted that "the ones common in all this land and all the year are like early figs. Others are as big as small pumpkins; ones with a big seed and little flesh and other with more flesh." Benavente was the first European to mention avocado leaf tea, noting that "the leaf is broad and very green; it has a very pleasant odor and water prepared from this leaf is good as a remedy for the legs and even better for the face."

The Spanish were so enthusiastic about the avocado that they brought seedlings to many of their other colonies in the Americas, the eastern hemisphere (Philippines and Indonesia) and Europe. In 1601, Valencia, Spain, became the site of Europe's first avocado tree.

Within one generation, Europeans had dispersed the avocado farther than the megafauna of the Pleistocene had been able to do in millions of years.

The English Discover the "Spanish Pear"

The first reference to an avocado in English occurs in 1589 by a British merchant named Hawkes, who had seen the fruit in Mexico. He called it an "alvacata." By the mid-1600s, Great Britain and other nations had begun establishing their own colonies in the New World. In 1655, they took possession of the former Spanish colony of Jamaica, where avocados had existed since the arrival of the Europeans, if not before.

In 1657, an anonymous author published *A Book of the Continuation of Foreign Passages* in London. In the chapter on Jamaica, the author mentions "avocatas," which he called a "wholesome, pleasant fruit; in season in August, and sold for eight pence per piece." In 1660, the British poet Abraham Cowley praised the "aguacata," along with other New World delicacies like cacao and tobacco. In Book Five of his Latin poem series dedicated to plants, trees and flowers, he wrote:

The Aguacat no less is Venus Friend
(To th'Indies Venus Conquest does extend)

A fragrant Leaf the Aguacata bears,
Her Fruit in fashion of an Egg appears;
With such a white and spermy Juice it swells,
As represents moist Life's first Principles.

While Cowley's poem may be the world's first ode to an avocado, it is unlikely that he ever tasted the fruit about which he rhapsodized.

The earliest firsthand description of an avocado tree in English is by William Hughes—a physician accompanying the British fleet in Jamaica—in his book *The American Physitian* [sic]: *A Treatise of the Roots, Shrubs, Plants, Fruit, Trees, Herbs, Etc. Growing in America*, published in London in 1672. Hughes's account includes the world's first written recipe for guacamole:

> *This is a reasonable high and well-spread tree, whose leaves are smooth, and of a pale green colour; the Fruit is of the fashion of a Fig, but very smooth on the outside, and as big in bulk as a Slipper-Pear; of a brown colour, having a stone in the middle as big as an Apricock, but round, hard and smooth; the outer paring or rinde is, as it were, a kind of a shell, almost like an Acorn-shell, but not altogether so tough; yet the middle substance…is very soft and tender….I think it to be one of the most rare and most pleasant Fruits of that Island…. [T]he Pulp being taken out and macerated in some convenient thing, and eaten with a little Vinegar and Pepper or several other ways, is very delicious meat.*

A 1697 account by British explorer, pirate and author William Dampier repeats the myth of "avogato pear" as an aphrodisiac but combines it with a dash of jingoism: "It is reported that the fruit provokes to lust, and therefore is said to be much esteemed by the Spaniards." His guacamole recipe is more detailed than that of Hughes's and includes the addition of lime, cilantro and onions, all of which the Spanish introduced to the Americas:

> *This* [avocado] *has no taste of itself, and therefore 'tis usually mixed with sugar and lime juice, and beaten together in a plate; and this is an excellent dish. The ordinary way is to eat it with a little salt and a roasted plantain; and thus a man that is hungry, may make a good meal of it.*

In 1696, the British naturalist Sir Hans Sloane became the first to print the name that much of the English-speaking world would use from that point on: avocado. However, he would also use another popular term:

The American Physitian;
OR,
A TREATISE
OF THE
ROOTS, ⎫ ⎧SHRUBS,
PLANTS, ⎬ ⎨FRUIT,
TREES, ⎭ ⎩HERBS, &c.nce

Growing in the

ENGLISH PLANTATIONS
IN
AMERICA.

Deſcribing the Place, Time,
Names, Kindes, Temperature,
Vertues and Uſes of them, either
for Diet, Phyſick, &c.

Whereunto is added

A DISCOURSE
OF THE
CACAO-NUT-TREE,
And the uſe of its Fruit; with all the
ways of making of CHOCOLATE.

The like never extant before. By *W. Hughes.*

London, Printed by *J. C.* for *William Crook*, at
the *Green Dragon* without *Temple-Bar*, 1672.

William
Hughes's
1672 book
on the flora
and fauna of
the Americas
includes
the earliest
firsthand
description of
the avocado
in English.
*Courtesy of the
Folger Digital
Collection.*

"alligator pear." In his catalogue of the plants of Jamaica, Sloane made the following brief entry in Latin: "The Avocado or Allegator [*sic*] Pear-Tree. It grows in gardens and fields throughout Jamaica." Thirty years later, Sloane would examine the avocado more thoroughly in a chapter devoted to "The Albecato Pear Tree; Spanish, Abacado or Avocado."

By the end of the 1700s or early 1800s, avocados had spread to Africa, Asia, Australia, Hawaii and the Canary Islands. In 1751, a nineteen-year-old George Washington accompanied his half-brother, Lawrence, to the West Indies to help the latter treat his tuberculosis. The trip shaped Washington in numerous ways. In his diary, he wrote that he developed a taste for "avagado pair." Thus, one of the earliest mentions of an avocado by a resident of the American colonies happened to be by a person who would become one of the most famous Americans who ever lived.

Yet despite Washington's cravings, it would be another century before the first commercial avocado groves were planted in the United States.

....

Grapefruit and Avocado Salad
By Rob Crisell

The Spanish introduced citrus into the New World soon after their arrival, but the new hybrid called grapefruit didn't come into being until the 1700s. By the time the grapefruit got to Florida in 1823, it had already been growing for several decades in Mexico. It's plausible that a Spaniard or a Native with epicurean tendencies was the first to create a version of this delicious marriage of European and Mexican fruits. In the 1980s, my mother used to make this dish using Fuerte avocados and Ruby Red grapefruits from our property.

INGREDIENTS
2 medium Ruby Red grapefruits, cut into ½-inch pieces
1 teaspoon finely grated grapefruit zest
2 tablespoons minced shallots
1 teaspoon white wine vinegar
2 medium California avocados, sliced ¼ inch thick
Coarse salt

2 tablespoons extra-virgin olive oil
Freshly ground pepper
Optional: 1 tablespoon Dijon mustard

Remove the flesh of the grapefruit, cutting in between the membranes to release the sections. Squeeze the juice from the membranes into a bowl. Transfer 2 tablespoons of the juice to another bowl. Add the zest, shallot and vinegar. Let the dressing stand for 10 minutes. Season the avocado with coarse salt and arrange on plates with the grapefruit sections. Stir the oil (and mustard if desired) into the dressing; season with salt and pepper. Drizzle onto the grapefruit and avocado. Adorn the salad with small edible flowers, such as nasturtiums, honeysuckle, lilacs or pansies.

COMING TO AMERICA

1800-1915

Whoever you are, wherever you live, let me say, give attention to the Avocado....
It will be a wonderfully pleasant occupation and a few acres will yield you a
generous income....We believe the Avocado to be the most valuable fruit known
to horticulture.
— from an advertising pamphlet for West India Gardens, 1915

While it may seem as though avocados have always existed in California, it took more than three hundred years after the arrival of Europeans to the New World before the first seedling found its way to the Golden State.

California was among the final frontiers for European explorers. The first Spanish expeditions to Alta California under Gaspar de Portolá and Franciscan missionary Junípero Serra didn't begin until 1769, roughly 150 years after the conquest. Interestingly, avocados were not among the many fruits, vegetables and grains that Serra and the rest of the company brought to California. Since the avocado had already been part of New Spanish cuisine for more than a century, it is unlikely that the missionaries simply forgot to bring them. Some speculate that the fruit's reputation as an alleged aphrodisiac may have played a role. Alternatively, it may have been that the missionaries—many of whom were agrarians and botanists—felt that California's arid climate would not support a semitropical fruit with significant water requirements. Whatever the reason, there is no evidence of avocados at any of the California missions.

In 1826, Eliza P. Reid provided an early—and inadvertently amusing—written description of an avocado in her *Historical and Literary Botany: Containing the Qualities, Anecdotes, And Superstitions, Relative to Trees, Plants, and Flowers, Which Are Mentioned in Sacred and Profane History*. Here is an excerpt from Reid's entry on "The Persea," which she helpfully identifies in a footnote as the avocado or "avogato pear":

> *The flower of the persea is of the rose species. The beauty of the tree…first caused the mysteries which the Egyptians attached to it. They consecrated it to Isis: they adorned the heads of their idols with its fruit; sometimes whole, and at other times opened, to show the kernel within.…All the ancient writers speak of this tree: Plutarch, Pliny, and Galen. It is said to have been planted at Memphis, by Perseus, who gave it his name.*

Reid's fanciful narrative demonstrates the world's widespread ignorance when it came to avocados, even a century after the first English accounts.

Avocados in Florida

Many historians credit Henry Perrine, a Floridian by way of New Jersey and Illinois, as the first person to introduce the avocado to the United States. However, there is no evidence for this popular myth. (There is even less evidence for the oft-repeated claim that the globe-trotting botanist David Fairchild did so in the late 1800s, although he did make the felicitous observation that avocados are "the veritable food of paradise.")

In 1827, Perrine—a physician and amateur botanist from New Jersey—was appointed as U.S. consul to Campeche, Mexico. His main task was inspecting cargo intended for the United States from the busy port of Tabasco. In 1828, the U.S. Department of Treasury tasked all consuls to find useful plants and seeds in their stations. Perrine seemed to be the only one to heed the call. Over a period of a decade, he shipped seventy plant specimens to friends and fellow horticulturalists in the United States. He sent more than one hundred boxes of botanical samples to John Dubose, a friend living in Key Biscayne. According to Perrine's list, these samples included the key lime and the avocado.

Perrine hoped to start a business importing tropical plants with Dubose when he finished his work in Mexico. To that end, he and his friends applied for a land grant in an area near Biscayne Bay. Around 1838, Perrine returned to Florida, moving with his family to a house on Indian Key, a village in the upper Florida Keys, where he waited for the new land grant to be surveyed. Unfortunately, members of a Seminole raiding party killed him in 1840, although his family escaped.

While Perrine cannot take credit for introducing avocados to America, his adopted state of Florida was undoubtedly the site of the country's first avocado plantings (although one could make a case for Hawaii as well), probably in the late 1700s. According to Jonathan Crane of the University of Florida Tropical Research and Education Center, avocados existed in South Florida well before the arrival of the first English-speaking settlers. "When settlers came to South Florida in the mid-1800s," he wrote, "they found avocados growing, probably introduced by indigenous people from the Caribbean." These avocados would have been West Indian types, since the salty soils and tropical climate of the Caribbean islands were (and still are) largely unsuitable for Guatemalan or Mexican varieties. Still, Florida's unpredictable growing conditions—its periodic deep freezes, destructive hurricanes and bad soils—inhibited the development of widespread avocado cultivation.

Luckily, a newly admitted state on America's still lightly settled Pacific Coast would prove to be the ideal home for the world's first truly successful avocado industry.

CALIFORNIA WELCOMES THE AVOCADO

In 1847, Mexico formally ceded Alta California to the United States in the Treaty of Cahuenga. Three years later, President Millard Fillmore signed the bill granting California statehood. In the mid-1800s, the new state was home to 150,000 Indigenous peoples and roughly 14,000 inhabitants of European and Mexican descent, most of whom lived around Monterey and Los Angeles. Due to this new state's isolated position between the Pacific Ocean to the west and the Sierra Nevada Mountains to the east, few Americans knew much about it. Even fewer wanted to live there.

That changed in 1848 with the discovery of gold at Sutter's Mill near Sacramento, California. By 1849, the California Gold Rush was drawing thousands of new immigrants from the East Coast and the world to the state. In 1845, San Francisco had fewer than 400 residents. By 1860, there were 56,000, with a total state population of 379,000, a 300 percent increase. The Golden State would continue to see net population gains for the next 160 years.

Judge Robert B. Ord became one of the state's first avocado growers when he planted three seedlings at his home in Santa Barbara in 1871. *Courtesy of SBC/THL.*

Meanwhile, a gold rush of a horticultural sort was taking place in the southern part of the state. No one knows who planted the first avocado in California, or where or when that person planted it. In 1964, Walter Beck and Jack Shepherd of the California Avocado Society (hereafter CAS, or "the Society") argued that Henry Dalton grew the first trees in the early 1850s at his ranch in what is now the city of Azusa. Even today, very old avocado trees still grow on a portion of Dalton's historic holdings, which Art Vasquez and his family have owned since 1958.

The first written reference to the avocado tree is in a report of the Visiting Committee of the California State Agricultural Society in 1856, in which the members discussed a visit to Dr. Thomas J. White at his home near San Gabriel in Los Angeles. They noted that "Dr. White has imported from Nicaragua a variety of choice tropical fruits including the sapote, the Aguacate or Butter Fruit, and the Mango." White's trees apparently did not survive.

Judge Robert B. Ord of Santa Barbara may be the state's first successful backyard grower. In 1871, Ord planted three avocado seedlings that he had brought back with him from Mexico. At least one tree remained productive until 1903. Many growers used seeds from his avocados to plant their own trees in Santa Barbara and the surrounding areas.

Kinton Stevens likely planted the state's first avocado grove in Montecito in the 1890s, not far from Ord's house. In the 1916 edition of the Society's annual yearbook (hereafter the "CAS yearbook"), Ira Condit—one of the industry's founders and early academics—quotes a letter from Francesco Francheschi, an Italian banker and innovative horticulturist who helped introduce two hundred new plant species to California. Francheschi wrote that Stevens laid out "the first orchard of Ahuacates ever planted in California." The grove was "set out in 1895 and comprised about 120 trees, all Mexican seedlings, which in a few years grew to considerable size." Francheschi reported that soon after Stevens died in 1897, his avocados met the same fate.

Another early avocado enthusiast was Juan Murrieta, the deputy sheriff of Los Angeles and namesake of the city of Murrieta. When he was seventy-four years old, Murrieta wrote an article for the 1918 CAS yearbook. He recounted that a friend "who has travelled much" gave him an avocado seed in 1871. Murrieta planted it at his home at College Street in Los Angeles. Later, he established a correspondence with a grower in Atlixco, Mexico, who began to ship him seedlings and avocados via rail.

On November 17, 1897, an article appeared in the *Pasadena Daily* describing Murrieta's cultivation of the "alligator pear," which was clearly still a novelty. The reporter—who never uses the term "avocado"—wrote that Murrieta "has demonstrated that a valuable food product, practically unknown in this latitude, can be successfully and profitably grown in Los Angeles County." He noted that Murrieta has a tree "in full bearing" that produced two hundred "perfect pears, worth

Juan Murrieta planted avocado seedlings from Mexico at his home in Los Angeles in the early 1870s. *Courtesy of Rebecca Farnbach.*

at retail in the San Francisco and Los Angeles markets $135." This is one of the first mentions in print of the avocado as a potentially lucrative food crop.

By the end of the century, avocado trees had spread throughout Southern California, including Escondido (W.W. Prior in 1892) and Orange County (Charles P. Taft in 1899).

Outside California, the vast majority of Americans had never heard of an avocado, let alone tasted one. Even the name "avocado" would not become a common part of the English lexicon until the middle of the twentieth century. In the early 1900s, "alligator pear" was perhaps the most popular name. Among other monikers were "avocat," "alvacata," "midshipman's butter," "poor man's butter," "butter fruit," "avocado pear" and "ahuacate." In 1905, American botanist Guy Collins, working for the Department of Agriculture, published one of the first comprehensive studies of the fruit titled *The Avocado: A Salad Fruit from the Tropics*. His monograph includes a chapter describing how ordinary people around the world typically prepare and consume avocado, along with several avocado-themed recipes.

In the three decades after Murrieta's first avocado tree, Los Angeles County experienced the most explosive period of expansion in its history. With the arrival of the Santa Fe Railway in 1885, the city and its surrounding suburbs now had a direct line to the East Coast. The county's population quadrupled

Researcher Raquel Folgado stands in front of a giant avocado tree planted by William Hertrich in 1906 at Henry Huntington's estate in San Marino. The Huntington Botanical Gardens are still home to several specimens from the state's first commercial avocado grove. *Photo by Rob Crisell.*

in the 1880s and then doubled again by 1900 to 170,000 residents. Over the next six decades, California would continue to see high double-digit growth, especially in the south.

In 1906, railroad magnate Henry Huntington planted California's first commercial avocado orchard. Huntington owned substantial real estate interests around the state and was an avid booster of Los Angeles. Horticulture was one of his passions. He allegedly sourced avocado seeds from a chef at the exclusive Jonathan Club in downtown Los Angeles, hiring nurseryman William Hertrich to plant four hundred trees at his palatial estate in San Marino. Subsequent arborists grafted over most of the young trees to different varieties as they grew. Today, a few of the original trees still thrive on the estate, which is now part of the Huntington Library, Botanical Garden and Art Museum.

By the end of the nineteenth century, California was already well known for its citrus, importing oranges, lemons and grapefruits around the country. By 1901, more than 4 million citrus trees had been planted in Southern

California. However, a few enterprising businessmen had their eye on a potentially bigger cash crop.

So-called nurserymen or propagators were the first to exploit what they saw as the vast economic potential of the avocado. These entrepreneurs were marketers and businessmen as much as they were horticulturists. The *Pacific Rural Press* reported in 1888 that one catalogue from the turn of the century featured 500 varieties of fruit trees, 700 ornamental shrubs and 270 roses. By 1901, horticulturists were propagating the avocado by budding and grafting, rather than planting seeds, which had proved ineffective. A few small nurseries began experimenting with the fruit, adding it to their repertoire of citrus, grapevines, cotton, stone fruit, olives and nuts.

Well-known propagators such as Charles Taft, E.E. Knight, F.M. Blake and A.R. Rideout were some of the earliest and most eager champions of the avocado. They were not afraid to proclaim—and, at times, wildly exaggerate—the virtues of this new crop. Along with real estate developers, propagators helped turn hundreds of hobbyists and wealthy landowners into full-blown commercial growers.

WILSON POPENOE AND THE HUNT FOR THE PERFECT AVOCADO

Perhaps the most important of these early avocado propagators were Frederick O. Popenoe and his son Wilson, a precocious young man from Alta Dena with a passion for the many new tropical and subtropical plants arriving in the state. The Popenoes would play a key role in turning California's infatuation with the avocado into a multimillion-dollar industry.

In 1904, after a career in real estate and publishing, Frederick Popenoe relocated his young family from Kansas to Southern California. While it is unclear when the elder Popenoe caught the "avocado fever," he quickly became one of its earliest and most ardent proponents. In 1910, he started West India Gardens at his property in Alta Dena, then a rural community fifteen miles northeast of Los Angeles in the foothills of the San Gabriel Mountains. As its name implies, his nursery specialized in the importation and cultivation of new tropical and semitropical fruits from Latin America and the Caribbean.

The fruit trees that Popenoe and other nurserymen introduced to California would have made Henry Perrine proud. Some would prove impossible to grow commercially, such as the feijoa, passion fruit, cherimoya,

A young Wilson Popenoe readies himself for avocado exploring. From 1916 to 1924, Popenoe traveled throughout Central America searching for new types of avocados. *Courtesy of SBC/THL.*

sapote, loquats, guava and mangos. Others would become significant cash crops for the state, such as dates and tomatoes. However, West India Gardens became best known for one tree in particular: the avocado.

One motivating factor behind Popenoe's decision to go into the nursery business may have been his youngest son, Wilson. Born in 1892, Wilson took an early interest in exotic plants. In high school, he corresponded with botanists in Europe and elsewhere. In 1910, he entered Pomona College, where he studied botanical sciences for a year.

In 1911, Wilson wrote "The Development of the Avocado Industry" for the *Pomona College Journal of Economic Botany*, the first of many academic pieces he would publish during his long life. In a paper sprinkled with quotes from his interviews with growers in Florida and California, Popenoe argued that Florida's relative success with avocado cultivation—despite that state's challenging growing conditions—demonstrated that California could not only grow the fruit on a wide scale but also become the dominant player. Young Popenoe was among the first to observe that the superiority of the Mexican and Guatemalan varieties—nearly impossible to cultivate in Florida—gave California a critical advantage over Florida's less appetizing West Indian varieties.

The only obstacle remaining, wrote Popenoe, was to develop or find the perfect variety through selective breeding and "agricultural exploration":

> *At the present moment the question of greatest importance to prospective avocado growers is "What are the best varieties for commercial purposes?" We have as yet no standard varieties, and it will be well, therefore, before the industry becomes established, to consider the characteristic required…and to obtain only those that come nearest to the ideal in every respect.*

Popenoe listed ten characteristics to consider in selecting a viable avocado variety: seasonality ("To obtain for this climate a set of varieties that will provide fruit of good quality…throughout the year"), hardiness, yield, size ("A mistaken idea…is that the larger the fruit the better"), form, uniformity, color, skin ("A good tough skin will cut down the loss of fruit in transit to the minimum"), seed and flavor ("A point which must be given first consideration"). For Popenoe, avocados possessing a high percentage of oil "are naturally the most desirable." This may have been an indirect swipe at Florida, but Popenoe may also have been targeting his fellow nurserymen and hobbyists, who were indiscriminately planting more than eighty different avocado varieties.

Wilson was not shy about promoting his family's West India Gardens in his article, referencing the company's efforts in Latin America to source "the most desirable fruits." He would himself soon embark on seven years of "avocado hunting" in Central and South America on behalf of West India Gardens and the U.S. Department of Agriculture. Wilson would maintain a lifelong connection to Honduras and Guatemala, living in Antigua for most of his life.

In advertising copy for their nursery, the Popenoes waxed enthusiastic about their favorite fruit. In a pamphlet from 1915, they described not just the avocado but also the lifestyle that it allegedly all but guaranteed:

> *Whoever you are, wherever you live, let me say, give attention to the Avocado. You may be a rancher. If so, and you have unoccupied land…plant it to Avocados. If you are not a rancher, but have a taste for growing things, and want a pleasant and very profitable occupation, plant avocados. You may be a city man who is tired of the city and wants to live and work in the country. Then investigate carefully and make the beginning intelligently for Avocado growing. It will be a wonderfully pleasant occupation and a few acres will yield you a generous income.…We believe the Avocado to be the most valuable fruit known to horticulture.*

Countless other nurseries, retailers and real estate agents would reiterate and embellish these sentiments over the coming decades.

FUERTE: CALIFORNIA'S FIRST BLOCKBUSTER VARIETAL

Probably one reason for Wilson's bullishness about the future of the avocado was that he knew that West India Gardens' employee Carl Schmidt had already found a number of candidates in Guatemala and Mexico that met the criteria outlined in his article.

In 1911, Frederick Popenoe had hired Schmidt after he left Cornell University, where he had studied agriculture. Since the nineteen-year-old Schmidt was the only employee who spoke Spanish, he was shipped off to Mexico to look for promising avocado varietals. Although he would work for West India Gardens for only a few years, Schmidt's discovery of the Fuerte—an avocado that would dominate the industry for the next sixty years—would cover him in glory until his passing at age seventy-eight.

When Schmidt arrived in Mexico City, there was no commercial avocado production. However, this did not deter the intrepid young man from his search. "In almost every dooryard is an avocado tree or two and they are to be found growing wild on the mountain-sides of areas climatically favorable to them," said Schmidt in an interview many years later. "It is from these scattered growths that the few avocados reaching Mexico City come. So the hunter of avocado budwood goes first to the market place."

After trying dozens of avocados in the vast markets of Mexico City, Schmidt found a specimen that seemed clearly superior to the others. He traced the fruit to the same town from which Juan Murrieta had sourced his seedlings forty years earlier. "Fortunately, I was able to learn where this pear-shaped, green, medium-size, oil-heavy, nutty-flavored specimen…came from," said Schmidt. "It was from Atlixco, a village not far distant. There in the backyard of a villager [Alejandro Le Blanc], I found the tree which is the parent of the California industry."

Eventually, Schmidt sent budwood of approximately thirty varieties to West India Gardens, including one labeled no. 15, which was the sample from Señor Le Blanc's yard. When the Popenoes received the buds, they began propagating them at their nursery. Neither the Popenoes nor Schmidt could have been overly optimistic about these agricultural explorations. Luckily for the California avocado industry, the state was about to experience an event that would reveal the potential of bud no. 15.

Alejandro Le Blanc poses with the parent Fuerte tree outside his house in Atlixco, Mexico. In 1911, Le Blanc allowed Carl Schmidt to ship Fuerte budwood to the Popenoes in Alta Dena. *Courtesy of SBC/THL.*

On January 5, 1913, a sudden polar vortex sent temperatures plunging across much of the western United States. Most of Southern California experienced low temperatures ranging from twelve to twenty five degrees Fahrenheit for several days. While healthy avocado trees can tolerate freezes of between thirty and thirty-two degrees, temperatures below thirty degrees for any amount of time seriously damage or even destroy trees, especially seedlings.

Since most of West India Gardens' stock were subtropicals, the 1913 freeze caused catastrophic losses, including most of Carl Schmidt's thirty avocados that Wilson had patiently grafted and raised. One seedling that survived was bud no. 15. The popular story goes that Frederick nicknamed the bud "Fuerte" (strong) because it had withstood the freeze. In 1940, however, Wilson explained that his father gave no. 15 the Fuerte moniker before the freeze because it was more vigorous than comparable buds. Regardless, no one knew yet whether Fuerte had any other positive characteristics besides its ability to survive a nasty freeze.

In March 1913, J.T. Whedon—a pig farmer who had been bitten by the avocado bug the year before—came to pick up forty trees that he had ordered from West India Gardens the previous spring. The Popenoes informed him that the freeze had killed his trees, along with $100,000 worth of other material, and that they had no money with which to reimburse him. They offered him the Fuerte seedlings, which were undersized and still non-bearing. Whedon reluctantly collected the plants and took them back to his farm in Yorba Linda.

When Whedon's grove bore fruit the subsequent year, the quality was remarkable. He began to receive orders from hotels and restaurants in Los Angeles and San Francisco for as much as twelve dollars per dozen avocados, an exorbitant amount at the time. Observers noted how prolific the trees were compared to other varietals. The yield was in some cases four thousand avocados per tree. After the Fuertes weathered another freeze in 1922, news spread about the hardiness, tastiness and precociousness of the new variety. Demand for Fuerte seedlings exploded. The Popenoes and West India Gardens had a smash hit on their hands.

Fuerte met nearly all of Wilson's criteria in his 1911 article, but it had some shortcomings. The variety eventually proved to be an inconsistent bearer. As John Coit—one of the industry's founders and scholars—pointed out in a 1968 article, "Each tree in the orchard has a different yield habit. A few are excellent bearers, some medium, but too many bear little or nothing although they grow side by side and appear equally healthy." Another

Grafted avocado trees in one of Popenoes' greenhouses at West India Gardens, circa 1920. *Courtesy of SBC/THL.*

complaint was that the Fuerte was not an ideal shipping fruit due to its thin green skin and its propensity to show bruises as it approached ripeness. Still, it was a vast improvement over any other avocado to date. By the mid-1940s, Fuerte dominated all new plantings, ultimately representing more than 70 percent of avocado production.

In 1915, however, there were still only one hundred acres of avocados in the entire state. At least growers now had an excellent, weather-resistant product and a promising, if still unproven, market. All they needed now was to marshal their collective enthusiasm, expertise and resources to create a full-blown industry.

....

Mexican Salad

Adapted from a pamphlet published by West India Gardens, 1913

Advertising pamphlets of West India Gardens and other nurseries often included recipes using avocados. Many involve little more than salt, pepper and lime. Others urged the liberal use of boiled eggs, Worcestershire sauce, gelatin, mayonnaise, sugar and other ingredients that would make modern foodies cringe. The following recipe from a 1913 West India Garden booklet is probably how many avocado aficionados in the early 1900s would have enjoyed their favorite fruit. I have modified it slightly for ease of use. (A photo of this recipe can be seen in the color section.)

INGREDIENTS
2 medium avocados, diced
½ medium sweet yellow onion, diced small
½ red bell pepper, diced small
½ mild green pepper (Anaheim, poblano, jalapeño, etc.), diced small
2 tablespoons olive oil
1 teaspoon white or apple cider vinegar
Salt and pepper to taste
Optional: diced tomatoes and squeeze of lime

In a bowl, dice two ripe avocados into ¼- to ½-inch pieces. Diced pieces should be firm enough to hold their shape. Add a half cup each of onion, red bell pepper and green pepper. Add diced tomatoes and a squeeze of fresh lime, if desired. In a separate bowl, combine two tablespoons of olive oil with one teaspoon of vinegar, along with salt and pepper to taste. Add oil mixture and mix together gently. Refrigerate for at least 1 hour before serving.

BIRTH OF AN INDUSTRY

1915-1925

Will the market take all that we are likely to raise? I think it will and it is the purpose of this Association to see that the public has no excuse for pleading ignorance of the great privilege which we are placing before it.

—Charles P. Taft, 1915

In 1914, there were still only a relative handful of avocado growers in California, mostly hobbyists with anywhere from one to a few dozen trees on their property. Hardly any of the state's 3 million inhabitants had even tasted the exotic fruit. Rare and costly, avocados were available only at specialty markets and high-end restaurants in big cities like Los Angeles and San Francisco. Avocado trees occupied fewer than one hundred acres, compared with more than twenty thousand acres of citrus in Orange County alone.

Nevertheless, passionate avocado advocates such as Coit, the Popenoes, Taft and others had seen the future, and it was green, nutritious and delicious. What avocado advocates lacked in numbers, they more than made up for in enthusiasm. They were wildly optimistic about the fruit's prospects in California and, indeed, the world.

In a 1915 article for the *Pacific Rural Press*, Wilson Popenoe and his father expressed the kind of excitement typical of many avocado aficionados, then and now. "In the beginning I shall assume that the avocado has come to stay," they wrote. "It is not supposable that a delicious fruit of the highest food value, which is found to flourish over a wide range of territory in this state, will be other than increasingly and extensively planted."

For the Popenoes and others, the fruit was nothing short of miraculous—a potential solution to the Malthusian forces that some saw in the wake of World War I. As wartime food demand boosted U.S. agricultural exports, many CAS members felt that the potential of avocado's food value was far greater than any agricultural product that had ever existed, including meat.

However sanguine they may have been about the avocado's prospects, these early enthusiasts knew that without an organization to shape and lead their infant industry, future prospects were grim. In their state's short history, Californians had already witnessed several horticultural booms and busts, including the eucalyptus, olive and spineless cactus fads. Even the citrus industry had been plagued with problems early on, mostly due to a lack of leadership and quality control. For the state's growers and retailers, the need for a governing association had never been more urgent.

Founding the California Avocado Association

On May 15, 1915, a dozen or so ambitious Californians met at the Alexandria Hotel in Los Angeles to form an association for the "improvement of the culture, production, and marketing of the Ahuacate." While the meeting was open to anyone, most of the attendees likely knew one another, since the avocado world was still quite small.

The first order of business was to elect officers and directors from among the growers, scholars, nurserymen and businessmen in attendance. Some of them—the Popenoes, Rideout, Coit, Taft and Coolidge—were already established names in the fledgling industry. In the end, attendees elected Los Angeles real estate developer Edwin G. Hart as president. Hart and the Popenoes were old friends who had collaborated on different projects in the past.

After establishing bylaws and electing a nine-person board, members confronted the pesky issue of what to name their group. Should they call themselves the "ahuacate" or the "avocado" association? "Avocado" ultimately won out, although the group's first yearbook retained the "ahuacate" usage. They also agreed that *avocados* should be pluralized without an *e*. They set up headquarters in the Union Oil Building in downtown Los Angeles. The initial charter listed seventy-four members.

Five months later, the board held the first official public meeting of the California Avocado Association, again at the Hotel Alexandria. The agenda of the all-day meeting was impressive. Growers, scientists, retailers,

Above: Workers for Calavo Growers in the 1930s harvest avocados using ladders, bags and wooden crates. *Courtesy of SBC/THL.*

Left: The oldest and most respected journal for avocado research in the world, the California Avocado Society yearbooks have been published annually since 1915. *Courtesy of SBC/THL.*

nurserymen, nutritionists, chefs and others gave presentations on marketing, nutrition, varieties, cultural practices, potential competition and culinary matters. These topics would occupy the yearly meetings of the association for the next one hundred years. (In 1941, its members voted to change the group's name to the California Avocado Society.)

Lunch consisted of a number of avocado dishes "worthy of the fruit" they introduced. These included sliced avocados, "dainty avocado sandwiches," avocado cocktails and mixed salads. On display was a box of green-skinned avocados that someone had shipped to Chicago and back. They were still edible. President Hart's remarks at the meeting underscored the urgency of the group's mission: "The combining into association of the many nursery men, orchard growers, experimenters and scientists interested in this new industry makes it possible to accumulate, and hold accessible to members the result of the work of the various individuals. This will prevent duplication of endeavor and serious failures."

Cooperation was key. Hart reminded them of the lesson taught by the citrus industry, whose lack of early organization caused problems that took years to overcome. Some of these problems included planting on land ill-adapted for citrus, planting lesser varieties, unscientific methods used in the raising and handling of the fruit and the use of inferior market facilities. These were unforced errors that the young industry could not afford to make.

Another of the Society's purposes was to garner positive press for the industry and to educate the public. This meant reducing fraudulent claims related to avocado cultivation, which Hart said had attracted a "class of boomers" and "unscrupulous promoters" drawn to the supposedly easy profits generated by the fruit. John Eliot Coit, the horticulturist and longtime president of the Society, warned in a later yearbook about the "great danger of an irresponsible real estate element running into excessive exaggeration in their use of the avocado in selling indifferent lands."

Early real estate firms in Southern California were rife with such advertising. "Alligator pears are the most profitable fruit grown in the world," screamed the headline of a typical newspaper ad in 1916 for building lots in Los Angeles. "You can live in luxury on your income from one acre."

Nurserymen were often just as guilty as developers. A.R. Rideout, another original Society board member, routinely made inflated assertions in his advertising brochures, like this one from 1920:

> *Last summer our family saved over one-third of the butter bills and over one-half of our meat bill by having avocados to eat most of the time....I*

Above: One of Edwin G. Hart's ads for residential lots in Vista and La Habra Heights. *Courtesy of SBC/THL.*

Left: A large grower and the first president of CAS, Edwin G. Hart, promoted the "avocado lifestyle" as part of his real estate marketing. *Courtesy of SBC/THL.*

believe it is valuable not only as a food, but as a medicine…half the ailments of mankind will be done away with.

Another pamphleteer promised that avocados "will feed the millions and tickle the palates of kings." At the 1920 Society meeting, respected horticulturist D.W. Coolidge averred that "one hundred years from now history will record that the highest civilization will cluster around the sections where the avocado is grown," where the "happiest and most beautiful children will be those who make the avocado, instead of meat, their daily diet."

Even the Society's first president, Edwin Hart, was an avocado "boomer." As a prominent real estate developer, Hart used the glamor of avocado trees to help sell lots in his planned communities of North Whittier Heights, La Habra Heights and Vista. One ad blared, "Avocados—An Assurance of a Life Long Income!" Hart would put his money where his mouth was, planting more avocados than nearly anyone else in the state before his untimely death in 1939.

Another critical role of the Society was to compile a "complete report on today's meeting, one copy of which will be mailed free of charge to each member of this association." These compilations—or "yearbooks," as they were called—contained the results of the annual meetings, including committee reports, as well as many other presentations on useful topics relating to the industry. From its inaugural issue in 1915, the Society would publish a yearbook annually until 2014, when the journal became an online quarterly.

Obsessing Over Varieties

Frederick Popenoe was one of the presenters at the first Society meeting in 1915. His talk, titled simply "Varieties," marked the beginning of what would be the industry's century-long obsession to identify or develop ideal types of avocado for California. Popenoe called it "the most important problem… avocado growers face at the present time." Since different varietals matured at different times throughout the year, leaders felt that three or four types were necessary. In his speech, Popenoe named and briefly described all eighty-six current varieties, most of which his fellow growers had invented in the last decade.

At last, he arrived at the dilemma facing the young industry: "Of course, it is highly desirable that we test as many varieties as possible…but let us…avoid confusing the mind of the prospective planter by forcing him to choose between a horde of unknown sorts, some of which may be absolutely inferior. Let us keep this industry freed from the confusion caused by numberless varieties."

At the following Society meeting, Dana King, an executive with the California Fruit Growers Exchange—the cooperative association of citrus producers—picked up Popenoe's theme: "You should standardize your varieties…if you standardize your produce, you should adopt something in the nature of a brand that would stand for your Association, and which would mean a certain thing to the consumer." King noted that the citrus industry slayed the varietal dragon early on, settling on essentially two varieties—Navel and Valencia. The United Fruit Company did the same with bananas, moving from a polyculture with several varieties to a monoculture of one easily marketable type.

Despite such sage advice, the battle of the varietals would rage on for many years, even after the establishment of Fuerte.

CONTROLLING THE COMPETITION

Two other events occurred around the time of the Society's founding that would prove critical to the industry's development. The first had to do with Mexico, a potentially powerful foreign competitor. The other concerned neutralizing an earlier, more established domestic competitor in Florida. (Hawaii had been growing avocados commercially since the late 1800s, but the fruit rarely made it to the mainland.)

Keeping Mexico Out

California growers had been visiting Mexico regularly in search of exotic fruits since the early 1800s. Contacts among Californians and their counterparts in Mexico remained congenial throughout the first half of the twentieth century. Underlying this collegiality, however, was the understanding that Mexican growers posed little threat to California's avocado dominance.

In the 1915 yearbook, Wilson Popenoe wrote that "one cannot marvel at the lack of commercial avocado orchards in tropical America." He attributed this to two principal reasons. The first was the difficulty of breeding avocado trees asexually to obtain desirable varieties. The second was the overall absence of commercial ambitions or infrastructure in Mexico for the cultivation and export of any produce at all. "It takes energy and organization to develop a great avocado industry," opined Popenoe, "which have not been forthcoming in the tropics." Another safeguard for California was that fact that Latin Americans were voracious consumers of avocados, making them unlikely exporters, at least in the near future.

"After all these years are California and Florida going to step in and take the matter out of the hands of our tropical neighbors?" asked Popenoe rhetorically. "It appears so."

Popenoe's low opinion of the industriousness of the people of the "tropics" notwithstanding, he was correct that Mexico posed no threat to American avocado growers in the first part of the twentieth century. It would be fifty years before Mexico developed an industry capable of challenging that of California. But there was another reason why the Society was largely unconcerned about Mexico as a potential rival.

A year before the founding of CAS in 1915, the Federal Horticultural Board of the U.S. Department of Agriculture had placed a quarantine on the export of avocados from Mexico and other countries of Central America. Originally enacted in 1912, the Plant Quarantine Act established a new board with authority to regulate the importation and interstate movement of nursery stock and other plants "that may carry pests and diseases that are harmful to agriculture." Invoking these new powers, Acting Secretary of Agriculture B.T. Galloway in 1914 forbade the importation of all avocados from Latin America because of an "injurious insect known as the avocado weevil (*Hilipu lauri*)." Galloway deemed the law operable "pending further investigation of the avocado weevil and of possible means of disinfecting the seeds of the avocado." The legislation had no expiration date.

Some historians have noted that advocates behind the Plant Quarantine Act were less concerned with keeping pests or diseases out of the United States than with protecting domestic producers from foreign competition. Like similar laws of the late nineteenth and early twentieth centuries—when President William McKinley and others openly advocated for protectionist policies—the Plant Quarantine Act served as a "super tariff," blocking foreign produce and thereby maintaining high prices on domestic goods like avocados.

Nevertheless, the ban on Mexican avocados remained in place in one form or another for eighty-three years, until the passage of the North American Free Trade Agreement in 1997.

HOW AVOCADOS GET TO THE STORE

Members of the industry have harvested, processed and shipped California avocados in much the same way for nearly a century, although technological advances continue to improve quality and efficiency. Several videos online show an avocado's journey from the grove to the dining table. Calavo Growers and Mission Produce Inc. even created a pair of children's books illustrating the process. From harvest to packing, migrant laborers from Mexico or Central America perform most of the work. The five main steps in the process are as follows.

HARVEST: More than 90 percent of the state's avocados are Hass, which means California's peak avocado season runs from spring to late summer. Since fruit matures differently at different altitudes and regions in the state, harvesting can take place as early as January or as late as October. Minor varieties such as Reed, Carmen, Lamb, Fuerte and GEM may be harvested at different times throughout the year. Like bananas, avocados ripen only once they are picked. However, mature fruit can hang on the tree for several months or longer. Before harvesting, testing determines minimum maturity standards, a process regulated by state agencies in coordination with the California Avocado Commission (CAC). Workers harvest manually using ladders and picking poles. Fruit goes into large plastic bins and is taken as quickly as possible to the packinghouse.

COOLING: When avocados arrive at the packing facility, they are immediately cooled down to between forty and fifty-three degrees for twenty-four hours to remove "field heat" and slow the ripening process. Hydrocoolers, forced-air machines or cold rooms accomplish this. The fruit is then cleaned, sanitized and dried.

SORTING: After the cooling process, fruit is placed on conveyor belts to receive an initial sorting for quality by hand. Damaged, misshapen or diseased fruit is culled. Avocados then go through an optical sorter, which instantaneously determines grades. They are labeled and sorted by grade, size, country and whether they are organic or conventionally grown. Size is based on the number of avocados that can fit in a standard twenty-five-pound carton. Sizes run from 28 (13.75–15.70 ounces) to 84 (3.75-4.75 ounces), with 48 (7.5-9.5 ounces) and 60 (6.25-7.5 ounces) being most common.

PRE-RIPENING. Most retail and institutional customers prefer avocados that are ripe soon after arrival. This requires a controlled ripening process invented in the 1980s, as discussed in detail in the "Avocado Land Becomes Avocado World" chapter. Pre-ripening involves placing avocados in a ventilated room at sixty-five to sixty-eight degrees for twenty-four to forty-eight hours with a small amount of circulating ethylene. Most major California handlers own or lease pre-ripening facilities around the United States.

PACKAGING and SHIPPING. A combination of people and machines pack the fruit into trays or bags. These are placed into cardboard crates, which are put on pallets and stored in cold rooms or sent to retail stores, restaurants or wholesalers in refrigerated trucks.

Keeping Florida Out

Unlike those from Mexico, Florida avocados were a present threat to the success of California's industry. In the same 1915 article in which he dismissed Mexico as a viable competitor, Wilson Popenoe noted that "an entirely different state of affairs" existed in Florida. With a more than twenty-year head start on California, Florida's industry "has been built upon a more substantial and profitable basis." The state had approximately two hundred acres of bearing trees with an "equal area recently planted," roughly twice the amount in California. Florida was also shipping its avocados to "all parts" of the United States, including San Francisco and Los Angeles. By the early 1920s, Florida had two thousand acres of avocados, of which eight hundred acres were bearing. Growers were sending more than 90 percent of their fruit out of state.

On the other hand, Popenoe seemed heartened that avocados from Florida were almost exclusively of the West Indian type. Indeed, more than 95 percent of newly planted trees were the Trapp, which Popenoe noted was "not an especially choice avocado." He said that at least one Florida grower had begun grafting over to Guatemalan varieties, but Popenoe was rightly skeptical as to whether a non–West Indian varietal could survive Florida's problematic climate.

In general, California growers thought there was a marked difference between their avocados and those of Florida. As one CAS member put it after a visit in 1925, "The Florida avocado will never have a preference in the market over California because it has a flat, watery, insipid taste." Still, Florida already had packinghouses as well as marketing and distribution. This put California at a severe disadvantage. What could be done to narrow the gap?

The answer lay in a quality that has made avocados popular for thousands of years: their high fat content. Not every kind of avocado is equally flavorful or oily. One pronounced advantage that California had over Florida is its ability to cultivate Guatemalan- and Mexican-type avocados. West Indian varieties generally have significantly less oil than a typical Mexican or Guatemalan. Lower oil means a less appetizing avocado. Cut the fat, cut the flavor, as they say.

In his 1915 presentation on varieties, Popenoe mentioned the average oil content of some of the more popular California types. These included Taft (18 percent), Sharpless (16 percent), Lyon (17 percent), Azusa (21 percent) and Fuerte (18 percent), to name a few. (The Hass—a Mexican-Guatemalan hybrid with an average oil content of 15 percent or more— would not exist until 1935.) By contrast, Florida's top three most popular West Indian varieties at the time—Trapp, Family and Pollock—had an average oil content of below 8 percent. (Although nutrition research was in its infancy in the early 1900s, most people already believed that the fats in avocados not only made the fruit satiating and delicious but also were good for you. See the "Avocado Revolution" chapter for a detailed discussion of avocado nutrition.)

There is no evidence that the industry sought governmental protection from its Sunshine State competitors. However, in 1925—less than a decade after the Society's first meeting—California enacted the Fruit and Vegetable Standardization Act "to promote the development of the California fruit, nut and vegetable industry and to protect the state's reputation in state and interstate markets by establishing standard packages for certain products." The section relating to avocados established a minimum maturity requirement, mandating that "all avocados, at the time of picking, and at all times thereafter, shall contain not less than 8 percent of oil."

Less than a month after the law went into effect, seven different shipments of Florida avocados arrived in California. Deputies with the Horticultural

Commissioner's office rejected all seven for failing to meet the new 8 percent oil content test.

The new law infuriated Florida's growers. They argued that their West Indian and hybrid varieties may mature and be acceptable for marketing prior to reaching the 8 percent threshold. They also noted that an existing federal law called the Agricultural Adjustment Act already governed their industry, trumping California's legislation. Nevertheless, Florida did its best to live with the onerous new standards.

In 1959, a group of Florida growers finally sued California in federal court, arguing that the 8 percent standard unfairly restricted access of Florida fruit in violation of federal law. The suit was unsuccessful in the lower courts. When the case at last found its way to the U.S. Supreme Court, it narrowly lost again.

In 1973, more than fifty years after the passage of the Fruit and Vegetable Standardization Act, a federal court held that California was in the wrong and could no longer enforce the 8 percent rule against Florida growers, finding that it "arbitrarily and unreasonably burdens interstate commerce… by imposing a standard which is irrational as applied to Florida avocados." By then, however, it was too late—California accounted for 90 percent of U.S. avocados. Florida would never again be a serious competitor.

....

Avocado Ice Cream
From a recipe provided at the inaugural meeting
of the California Avocado Association, 1915.

At the first Society meeting, organizers provided various avocado-themed recipes to attendees, including this one for an easy, no-churn avocado ice cream. (If you have an ice cream maker, use it.) I have modified the recipe for ease of use. Avocado is also ideal for use in protein shakes.

INGREDIENTS
2 cups whole milk
2 cups heavy cream
5 egg yolks
Pinch of salt
2 cups sugar

1 teaspoon vanilla extract (and almond extract, if desired)
4 medium-sized ripe avocados
Maraschino cherries
Optional: Crushed bits of dark chocolate or freshly chopped mint leaves
Optional: Generous squeeze of lime

In a large pan, slowly cook the milk, cream, eggs, pinch of salt and 1 cup sugar until it is thick enough to coat the spoon. Remove from heat and flavor with vanilla extract. In a blender, combine the ripe avocados with the remaining cup of sugar. Cool the custard in the refrigerator for 2 hours and then blend it into the fruit mixture in a bread pan or similarly sized container and freeze. Serve in small bowls with a few cherries on top of each serving.

MARKETING THE ARISTOCRAT
OF SALAD FRUITS

1925-1940

This is a young and virile industry, characteristically American in spirit and entirely new in method. It is rapidly winning its way into American markets with an opportune product.

—John Eliot Coit, 1928

In forming the California Avocado Society in 1915, growers had taken the first step in ensuring what they hoped would be a long, profitable journey into the new century. Despite the optimism of its founders, though, the industry would not exist in any meaningful sense for at least another decade or so. However, as demand for avocados began to rise, "Avocado Land"—a term coined by future industry leader Jack Shepherd—would expand as quickly as the young state of California itself.

The 1920s saw spectacular growth in California, especially in the Greater Los Angeles area. In one decade, the City of Angels doubled in size from 600,000 people to 1.2 million. Jobs in agriculture, manufacturing and especially oil production attracted people from across the country. Agriculture was still drawing farm workers from the United States, Mexico and Asia, although oil had finally surpassed it as the state's leading industry. By 1930, the Los Angeles basin had thirty-two refineries employing 5,000 people. Growth paused momentarily with the onset of the Depression, but the build-up to World War II marked the beginning of yet another round of furious expansion.

FORMING THE CALAVO GROWERS EXCHANGE

In the first years of the industry, most growers found it relatively easy to market their own fruit without the aid of an assocation. Low supply and high demand meant buyers often paid as much as $0.75 per fruit, roughly $15.00 in today's currency. This led many speculators to try their luck in the avocado business, buying trees from West India Gardens and other nurseries. As thousands of newly planted trees entered production, prices began to decline as supply outpaced the ability of growers to market a still relatively expensive and unknown fruit.

To combat these problems, CAS formed a marketing department in 1921, contracting with American Fruit Growers, a large produce marketing company in Los Angeles. Unfortunately, the relationship ended within a year. This was partly due to a light avocado crop that year, but also because of what Hart, Coit and other industry leaders called "lack of cooperation." Many member-growers still sold their best fruit to old customers, while offering the new marketing company their lower-grade fruit. This arrangement worked in 1922, when there was only 150,000 pounds of avocados to market. However, the estimate for 1923 was for 560,000 pounds. That much fruit would need more than a borrowed marketing team and a half-committed membership.

In 1923, CAS recruited George B. Hodgkin, a former marketing executive with the California Fruit Growers Exchange (later renamed Sunkist Growers), to spearhead marketing and sales for the new industry. The Society tasked Hodgkin with forming a cooperative exchange for avocado growers similar to Sunkist. Working closely with the indomitable Coit—director of the Society from 1923 to 1947—Hodgkin became the first general manager of the California Avocado Grower's Exchange. After a national naming competition, the exchange rebranded itself as Calavo, a clever portmanteau word combining "California" and "Avocado." By 1924, Calavo Growers had taken over all marketing and handling of avocados. In its first year of operations, the exchange marketed 180,000 pounds of fruit from forty-six different avocado varieties, convincing most growers of its effectiveness. Hodgkin would go on to manage Calavo for the next thirty-three years.

Opposite: Botanist and industry leader John Coit was called the "Father of the California Avocado Industry." He served for years as CAS director, yearbook editor and director of Calavo. *Courtesy of SBC/THL.*

Above: George Hodgkin (*left*) and Albert Thille celebrate the twenty-fifth anniversary of Calavo, circa 1950. Hodgkin served as the exchange's first general manager, a position he held for more than thirty years. *Courtesy of SBC/THL.*

The creation of Calavo was as transformative for the young industry as the founding of CAS had been ten years earlier. The cooperative exchange would dominate marketing and distribution for the next four decades, competing with a handful of smaller independent packinghouses—or "handlers," as they are more commonly called—in La Habra Heights, Fallbrook, Escondido and elsewhere. Calavo's innovative marketing became a model for other produce marketers around the country.

As head of the exchange, Hodgkin was not afraid to push the industry and its growers to make changes when necessary. Standardization of fruit was at the top of his list. At the Society meeting of 1925, Hodgkin noted that the exchange was shipping too many kinds of avocado—the number was approaching two hundred. "Some of these varieties are not giving satisfaction on the local markets," he stated. There were too many "cats and dogs"—too much fruit of uneven quality. Hodgkin announced that Calavo would now accept "only" nineteen varieties of avocados—nine for shipment and local sales and ten more for local sales only. Calavo even began placing a hand-stamped trademark in yellow letters on each avocado. (The exchange abandoned this practice in 1937.)

The 1927 season marked the first million-pound crop in California, as well as the first rail shipments of avocados to Chicago and New York. The bumper crop sent prices plummeting, despite new advertising programs and expanded sales routes. One year later, the state saw a crop that was six times larger than the previous year and three times larger than any crop ever marketed. It was the first test for the young exchange, which had to market and sell a highly perishable, winter-spring fruit that only 10 percent of Americans had ever heard of. To make matters more challenging, Calavo sold mainly to high-end retail stores and restaurants, since those customers were more likely to appreciate—and afford—the still-pricey fruit.

Some growers didn't understand the difficulties of selling avocados. This would not change over the years. "The industry is very challenging operationally because of perishability," explained Rob Wedin, a sales executive who worked at Calavo for forty-nine years. "Most people didn't really know how this business works. It's way rougher, way faster, than people would think."

Founders such as the Popenoes and Hart felt that the avocado was the solution to a host of perceived modern ills, such as overpopulation and allegedly declining resources like meat and dairy. Others endorsed avocados for health reasons, echoing faddish health gurus like John Harvey Kellogg, who wrote that "of all edible fruits, the avocado stands pre-eminent as a source of concentrated nutrient adapted for human use."

CALAVO
THE ARISTOCRAT OF SALAD FRUITS

A Calavo ad from 1930. The exchange often used models and actresses in advertisements and promotions. *Courtesy of Calavo Growers.*

An example of Calavo's high-end marketing of its avocados in Los Angeles, circa 1930. *Courtesy of SBC/THL.*

"In the United States such a change is now in progress," wrote Coit in 1928. "Less bread and meat and more fresh fruits and vegetables is the order of the day, and the result is a marked improvement in the health of the nation."

"It takes the place of meat," proclaimed a fervent Society member at the 1918 meeting. "This is a slogan that will make many eat it....I asked an engineer employed on the canal if avocados were generally eaten in Panama and his reply was, 'There are five thousand whites in the City of Panama and if there is one who does not eat them he is a freak.'"

Progressive assumptions about the supposed inevitability of avocados may be why a salesman like Leigh Crosby—one of Calavo's early advertising executives—was often blunt in his advice to Society members. "We have to realize that there is nothing miraculous about our product. All we have is another highly perishable fruit for which there is no particular demand."

In the early years, salespeople in markets outside California routinely had to inform their potential customers what an avocado was, how to tell when it was ripe and how to eat it. Crosby said that when he conducted a survey of a large cooking school in Chicago in 1927, he discovered that "only about 2% of the women…had ever heard of avocados or alligator pears." He was proud to report that two years later, half of them were now familiar.

The reports of these early salesmen and their "Mad Men" advertising techniques make for amusing reading. Crosby said that he would regularly "bring pressure to bear" at hotels and restaurants that he and his colleagues visited during their sales trips. If they were in a restaurant that did not have avocados on the menu, Crosby would tell the manager, "We thought this was a first-class institution. If you haven't any Calavos, have you any broccoli or zukini [*sic*]?" (other "high-class" vegetables). He would then inform the waiter that he was "travelling around the country a good deal" and that the waiter "ought to….find out about the new things in the market."

Crosby called this technique the "appeal to style" or "class." In the first half of the twentieth century, Calavo salespeople developed three principal ways to sell avocados—"by appealing to the appetite, by appealing to style, or by an appeal to health." Since there were many cheaper fruits and vegetables that satisfied consumers demand for health and taste,

The Calavo packinghouse in Vista in 1934. This was the company's largest facility until the 1950s. *Courtesy of Calavo Growers.*

Crosby says that he and his colleagues "appealed primarily to their pride." Marketing strove to "class up" an already luxury item. The exchange staged photoshoots with film stars holding Calavo-branded avocados. They came up with slogans that underscored the class-conscious appeal, such as "The Aristocrat of Salad Fruits" or "California's exotic glamour fruit." Calavo salespeople even began substituting "Calavo" for generic names like "avocado" or "alligator pear."

Crosby concluded his 1925 talk with an admonition that both CAS and Calavo had to do more to teach consumers about the avocado so that they would pay a premium for it. To do this, a central organization was required to provide three necessary things: "a standardized product, brains, and money." The message was clear: future success for avocado growers depended on a united industry with creativity and a singular purpose. Or as a 1929 headline in a Calavo newsletter stated, "CALAVO is the ONLY HOPE."

Growers began to get the message. In 1928, Calavo had 338 members, but only 25 percent supplied the bulk of the marketed fruit. As large commercial plantings began to come into bearing and growers faced

A 1927 promotion for Calavo's "first shipment of avocados to Canada." *Courtesy of Calavo Growers.*

more competition, more people joined the cooperative. By 1937, Calavo was marketing about 80 percent of California's thirteen thousand acres of avocados.

Many of Calavo's marketing and sales efforts were quite innovative. Although avocado prices in the late 1920s would trend downward because of freezes, oversupply and the Depression, marketing was rapidly increasing avocado awareness among American consumers. In 1927, "Calavos" were delivered to President Calvin Coolidge at the White House ("Calavos Consumed by Coolidges at Capitol"). Hollywood stars gushed about growing avocado trees in their backyards. New avocado recipes received space in *Vogue* and *Better Housekeeping*. Although avocado nutrition studies would not exist until the 1980s, Calavo occasionally worked with scientists to write articles touting the fruit's health benefits.

As hoped, all this marketing increased demand, which inspired more landowners to get into the avocado game. Production rose from a few hundred tons in the early 1920s to well over twenty-one thousand tons by 1943. Hundreds of new groves appeared in Ventura, Santa Barbara, Orange, Los Angeles and San Diego Counties. Groves were often the centerpieces of an "avocado lifestyle" community, such as La Habra Heights and Vista, which former CAS president Edwin Hart developed in the 1920s.

Despite these efforts, most Americans in the mid-1930s still saw avocados as a luxury item at best or an oddity at worst. However, the fruit was at last making serious inroads into the national consciousness. Calavo sold most avocados in the western United States, but larger cities east of the Mississippi had limited quantities as well. The exchange sent out recipe booklets, educational pamphlets and grocery store displays. It ran ads in magazines, trade journals and newspapers. Between 1915 and 1927, food advertising grew by 570 percent in the United States.

As demand expanded, supply began to outpace it as usual, a pattern that would repeat itself many times over the next century. The 1934 crop reached 20 million pounds—a 400 percent improvement over the previous year. This glut sent prices crashing to $0.05 per pound. Still, Calavo continued to grow its sales and marketing force. The exchange soon had forty-five branches around the country, including Cleveland, Pittsburgh, Buffalo and Detroit. It started marketing other produce besides avocados, including dates, limes and dried fruit.

Coit was effusive in his assessment of his profession's first two decades. "This is a young and virile industry," he wrote in the 1928 yearbook, "characteristically American in spirit and entirely new in method. It is

A sorting line at a Calavo Growers facility in the 1930s. *Courtesy of SBC/THL.*

rapidly winning its way into American markets with an opportune product. It is already a justification for the faith of the founders of the California Avocado Association."

By the end of the 1930s, the avocado industry had survived the lean years after its founding, thrived during the Roaring Twenties and continued to prosper even in the Depression-era '30s. As the state's population exploded, avocado sales seemed poised to do the same.

CHALLENGES AHEAD

Not all was smooth sailing for the young industry. In their definitive timeline, Gary Bender and Jack Shepherd point to gathering clouds on the horizon, many of which would grow even darker in the coming decades.

Despite the ongoing quarantine on Mexican fruit, competition outside California did exist. While Florida no longer represented the threat it once did thanks to the Fruit Standardization Act, Cuba was exporting millions

KING FUERTE REIGNS SUPREME

Although Calavo could not convince Americans to make its name synonymous with avocados, it did persuade its members to plant fewer and better varieties. Eventually, the Fuerte variety dominated most new plantings across the state. This led to more consistent quality, which made the job of salespeople much easier. The freezes of 1913, 1922 and particularly 1937—which killed a third of that year's crop—spurred growers to "top work," replant or develop new groves with the more frost-tolerant Fuerte. It was also popular with consumers and retailers because of its high oil content, its pleasant nutty taste and its ability to ship. Growers planted Fuerte widely in San Diego County, which had become the central region for avocados in the state.

This did not mean that the industry had given up on developing new varieties. The Society continued to encourage breeding research at University of California–Riverside and its Cooperative Extension (UCCE). Many in the industry dreamed of being able to provide year-round avocados, which required varietals that matured in spring, summer and fall to supplement Fuerte, a winter fruit. The quest for a year-round supply would persist until Mexican exports began in the 2000s.

For the time being, however, Fuerte fulfilled all the criteria of a successful avocado variety. In the words of John Coit, this meant it could "bear well, look well, ship well and eat well." Despite some misgivings about the first and third criteria—the variety was an inconsistent bearer and it bruised easily in transit—Fuerte met Coit's other qualifications. In 1938, Fuerte represented 75 percent of California's crop and an even higher percentage of its nonbearing acreage. Of the nineteen or so avocados that Hodgkin identified as acceptable in 1925, commercial growers were only planting a few of them anymore. Fuerte was king.

In 1938, to mark the triumphant victory of Fuerte in the battle of the varietals, fifty or so CAS members traveled by train to Atlixco to honor Alejandro Le Blanc and Mexico's singular contribution to the state's avocado industry. It was on Le Blanc's property in 1911 that Carl Schmidt discovered the Fuerte "Parent Tree," sending buds back to the Popenoes in Alta Dena. Mexican and American dignitaries gave speeches. The Society awarded Le Blanc its first medal of honor for "outstanding

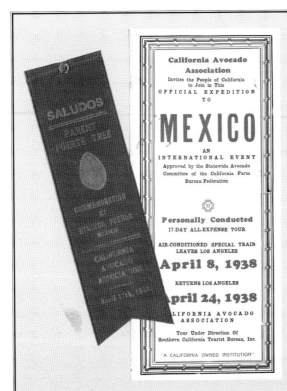

Ticket and ribbon commemorating the Society's 1938 "pilgrimage" to Mexico from Los Angeles to honor the original Fuerte tree and its owner. Courtesy of SBC/THL.

and meritorious service to the avocado industry." It also placed a plaque at the site to commemorate its "food fruit," which was deemed "full of goodness, quality, productivity, and other qualities necessary to command the esteem and interest of the scientific-commercial world." The 1938 yearbook featured eleven articles about the "pilgrimage."

Ironically, in the same yearbook anointing Fuerte as king, a committee report detailed "experimental varieties that should have further trial." One of these varieties was a hybrid patented a few years earlier by a California postman from La Habra Heights named Rudolph Hass. The editors described Hass's new variety as a "black fruit with leathery skin, very small seed and of high quality...with oil content over 20%."

None of the pilgrims in Atlixco could have predicted that Mr. Hass's obscure avocado would not only dethrone Fuerte within a few decades but also eventually enable Mexico to replace California as the most dominant avocado producer in the world.

of avocados into the United States. These imports mostly affected the profit margins of Florida growers, but they also worried Calavo and its members. In 1934, California and Florida lobbied Congress to place tariffs on Cuban fruit, which was on the duty-free list because of the Cuban Reciprocity Treaty. These efforts failed. Only when Castro took over the country in 1959 did the subsequent U.S. embargo finally block avocados from Cuba for good.

Pests and disease are constant threats to the welfare of any agricultural industry. Thankfully, the avocado is generally a hardy species, not prone to many of the problems afflicting other trees and crops. However, it is not bulletproof. Between 1928 and 1940, the most serious avocado pest in the state was a species of armored scale insect called latania scale (*Hemiberlesia lataniae*). Luckily, the insect was controllable with oil sprays or by using natural biological defenses such as ladybugs. With the high price of avocados, theft also became an issue. Bandits made off with entire harvests under the cover of darkness. Even today, theft remains a serious problem for growers. Chain link fences and security cameras are widely employed.

However, the most serious threat during this time was avocado root rot. In the 1930s, avocado farmers began noticing that many of their trees were dying, especially in San Diego County. "We have observed a number of avocado trees which have shown alarming decline, especially on hillside and bench land plantings in soils which are shallow or underlain with compact subsoil," wrote Marvin Rounds, the pioneering farm advisor for Los Angeles County in the 1939 yearbook.

Referred to at first as "tree decline," the problem was ultimately identified as "root rot." The infected tree shows signs of distress, defoliation and branch dieback occur and death usually follows within two years. Until 1942, Zentmyer and other researchers believed that soil factors such as poor aeration or waterlogged conditions caused root rot. In 1939, V.A. Wager, a visiting South African plant pathologist at the Citrus Experiment Station in Riverside, showed that poor soil conditions did not cause root but merely worsened them. He identified the real culprit as a pathogen called *Phytophthora cinnamomi*. Root rot was—and still is—incurable and rapid, resulting in death of the host tissue. The effort to eliminate the disease would occupy the industry for the next forty years.

. . . .

Calavonnaise
Adapted from the "Library of Calavo Recipes" pamphlet, 1937

In 1924, Calavo took over the duty of creating recipes for the industry. Over the next fifty years, the exchange would publish hundreds of recipes for avocado-themed dishes. One of the more popular offerings was a recipe for a spread made from avocados, cleverly called "Calavonnaise." The recipe here was adapted from a 1937 marketing brochure. Less caloric and more nutritious than traditional mayonnaise, this spread is worth trying the next time you're in the mood for a sandwich or burger.

INGREDIENTS
1 tablespoon lemon juice
¼ cup whole milk (or olive oil)
½ teaspoon salt or to taste
1 teaspoon mustard (Dijon style works well)
6 drops Tabasco sauce or to taste
1 medium-sized avocado, mashed
Optional: 1 teaspoon grated horseradish and/or 1 teaspoon white vinegar

Add lemon juice to milk or olive oil. Beat well. Add salt, mustard, Tabasco sauce and any optional ingredients, as desired. Add to mashed avocados. Beat well by hand or in blender until it has a mayonnaise-like consistency. I find that using olive oil creates a lighter and more appetizing spread.

THE COMMERCIAL ERA BEGINS

1940-1960

Like the growing of them, the marketing of avocados has been achieved under "impossible" conditions....But effective marketing was achieved—largely because growers worked together with an almost evangelistic fervor.
—Jack Shepherd, 1952

After founding the marketing association known as Calavo Growers in 1924, the industry grew rapidly. By 1940, production was approaching 50 million pounds per year on more than fourteen thousand acres around the state.

Besides the virtues of the avocado itself, the untiring efforts of the leaders and members of the two associations spurred on the industry. John Coit was the most important of these early leaders. From 1915 to 1947, Coit—CAS president, accomplished botany professor, sixteen-year editor of the Society's yearbook and the founding director of Calavo—shaped the avocado industry with his formidable intelligence and genial leadership. "Dr. J. Eliot Coit is truly 'The Father of the California Avocado Industry,'" wrote the editors of the 1939 yearbook. "From its babyhood…when growing avocados was a hobby, through adolescence…as a full-fledged industry Dr. Coit has been its able and watchful parent."

For thirty years, no one rivaled Coit's influence. When he stepped away from active leadership in the mid-1940s, many must have wondered whether anyone would be able to fill the void. Thankfully, another remarkable person was ready to do exactly that.

JACK SHEPHERD AND THE RISE OF CALAVO

From his humble beginnings in 1933 as a twenty-year old Calavo publicist until his death in 2006 at age ninety-two, Jack Stickney Shepherd dedicated his life to the avocado industry. A graduate of Pasadena Junior College, Shepherd succeeded Coit as the CAS yearbook editor, a title he would hold for forty-eight years. He also served as CAS president for many years and held various positions at Calavo, including president. He was also instrumental in creating the California Avocado Commission and is one of only four people to receive the Society's annual Award of Honor twice. A prolific writer, persuasive speaker, happy warrior and meticulous archivist, Shepherd shaped and guided his beloved industry in countless ways. Today, the Shepherd-Brokaw Collection at the Huntington Library—painstakingly curated by Shepherd and Carl Stucky over many years and donated on behalf of the Society in 2010—stands as a fitting legacy to Shepherd's years of devotion.

In 1952, Shepherd—then an assistant field manager at Calavo and CAS secretary—delivered a keynote speech at the Society's annual meeting. Using *Alice in Wonderland* as his theme, Shepherd was at turns exhortatory and prophetic as he assessed the past, present and future of Avocado Land:

> *When Lewis Carroll's Alice stepped through the mirror into the "Looking-glass World," she discovered, I might suggest, a place that is strangely reminiscent of "Avocado Land."…We have taken a tree that Nature didn't intend to grow here, and we have planted it….But the trees grow, and produce fruit….It seems more like a "Looking-glass" fruit—more like a vegetable growing on a tree. But it's wonderful.*
>
> *Like the growing of them, the marketing of avocados has been achieved under "impossible" conditions. The fruit was almost totally unknown in this country when it was first introduced commercially….The first great crops occurred in the depths of the Great Depression….But effective marketing was achieved—largely because growers worked together with an almost evangelistic fervor.*

By 1952, the avocado industry was growing as fast as California itself. While the state's remarkable expansion in the 1920s slowed in the post-Depression years of the 1930s, both it and its young avocado industry regained their momentum in the years leading up to World War II. Within two decades after 1940, California doubled in population, from 7 million

In 1935, a twenty-two-year-old Jack Shepherd (*right corner*) works at his desk in the Calavo packinghouse in Vista. Shepherd was the industry's most fervent advocate and leader until his passing in 2006. *Courtesy of Calavo Growers.*

to 15 million. The avocado industry underwent a comparable expansion. Plantings rose from roughly 14,000 total acres in 1937 to 16,300 in 1945 to 26,000 by 1957. In 1942, gross returns exceeded $3 million, with more than 12,000 tons harvested. By the late 1950s, production had ballooned to 50,000 tons.

Nevertheless, the two decades between 1940 and 1960 were often tumultuous. Thanks to Fuerte's inconsistent bearing, crop production could vary greatly from year to year. Other factors affecting consistent production included the age distribution of trees, weather conditions and technology. This meant prices tended to fluctuate wildly. In 1940, the average wholesale price plunged to just $0.05 per pound. Over the next twenty years, prices would rise and fall but would average only $0.15 per pound.

Despite the rocky ride, Shepherd and the members of the Society and Calavo felt that the industry was heading in the right direction. The

A state-of-the-art Calavo Growers' packing line from 1948. *Courtesy of SBC/THL.*

exchange's innovative and aggressive marketing had led to much broader awareness of avocados among ordinary Americans. The exchange still sold the avocado as a luxury item—a 1953 Calavo advertisement called it "California's exotic glamour fruit"—but it was more accessible and cheaper than ever. Thanks to Calavo's marketing, many now thought that avocados were not only delicious but also nutritious. Images of happy children accompanied ads, letting parents know that the fruit was "recommended by pediatricians for infant and child feeding." Nearly all ads in the 1940s and 1950s reminded readers of the fruit's many vitamins and minerals, as well as its "linoleic acid for youthful vigor."

Per capita consumption rates rose steadily. The first wave of commercial Mexican restaurants in the 1940s also helped drive demand. The federal

The City of San Diego sponsored a "Vista Calavo" float at the 1932 Rose Parade in Pasadena. *Courtesy of Los Angeles Times Photographic Archive, UCLA Library Special Collections.*

government identified avocados as a cheap and nutritious way of feeding the troops overseas and around the country, as well as citizens living on war rations back at home. A 1944 booklet called *Calavo on Your Wartime Menus* states:

> *Calavo avocados are plentiful. Unrationed! And their rich nutritional values recommend for a top-spot on wartime menus. They help "stretch" meat points…They help "stretch" butter points.…Enjoy Calavos as often as you like. There are so many ways—served alone as a half-shell…as a spread for war workers' lunches…to replace rationed canned fruits…for "he-man" salads…entrees…desserts.*

But the industry was experiencing growing pains as well—among them the combined threats of urbanization, rising farming costs, unstable crop prices, uneven production and root rot. By the mid-1950s, some growers had begun to question Calavo's commitment and competence. Independent packinghouses had always existed, but they now began to multiply, especially in San Diego County. Calavo saw its share of the market shrink from roughly 80 percent in 1950 to around 60 percent by 1960.

While these growing pains had much to do with changes in industry practices, their effects on growers depended greatly on where they lived. California's avocado districts took on certain distinct "personalities" that remain remarkably consistent even through the present day.

THE "PERSONALITIES" OF CALIFORNIA'S AVOCADO DISTRICTS

Until the 1980s, Avocado Land was divided into three main districts and dozens of subdistricts: the northern counties (Santa Barbara, Ventura and San Luis Obispo), the mid-counties (Los Angeles, Orange, Riverside and San Bernardino) and San Diego County (Fallbrook, Pauma-Pala Valley, Escondido and Vista). While all three districts boasted of avocado plantings as early as the late 1800s, most groves were in the south. The two decades between 1940 and 1960 would see a gradual decline of groves in the mid-counties, a steady expansion of plantings in the northern counties and the emerging dominance of San Diego County.

Mid-Counties

While most early avocado development in California until the 1920s occurred in Los Angeles County, new plantings had shifted to La Habra, Fullerton and other more rural communities in Orange County by the 1930s. By the 1950s, urbanization had made new grove development in these areas cost-prohibitive, as developers removed avocado groves to make room for new housing and retail. Still, some five thousand acres remained even into the mid-1960s, primarily smaller groves owned by physicians, dentists and business executives. When the ten-acre restrictions on lots in places like San Gabriel Valley, La Habra and Irvine Ranch expired in the 1970s, there was an explosion of housing developments, along with steep increases in taxes, water costs and land values. By 1966, only three thousand acres remained in the mid-counties. A decade later, nearly all the large groves were gone, replaced with housing tracts and commercial centers.

Northern Counties

Although Santa Barbara is the traditional birthplace of avocado production in the state, cultivation began slowly in the northern counties, with fewer than one thousand acres by 1945. While there were many more established groves and professional farmers than anywhere else in Avocado Land, citrus was the crop of choice. Over the next twenty years, avocado plantings in the Ventura-Fillmore area would slowly surpass those of the mid-counties, rising to seven thousand acres by 1970. Still, expansion in the northern counties would remain modest until well into the 1980s. It would not be until 2010 that plantings would finally surpass those in the south, a process discussed in detail in the "Avocado Revolution" chapter.

San Diego County (Escondido, Fallbrook, Pauma/Pala Valley and Valley Center)

San Diego County became the beating heart of Avocado Land by 1950. Its rural, northern subdistricts dominated the American market for the next five decades. Growers first cultivated avocados in San Diego County in the late 1800s. In a 1926 CAS article, Frederick Popenoe observed that there were already 1,200 acres—half the state's total at the time—in the county. Most groves were small and located in coastal communities like Vista, Carlsbad and Encinitas. He predicted that the "future of the industry in that county is bright," stating that there would be a "healthy and large increase in acreage…probably the largest in the entire state."

It did not take long for Popenoe's prediction to come true. By the late 1940s, San Diego County dominated all districts in the state, with more than two-thirds of total avocado acreage. Initially, most new plantings were in Vista, an area that real estate speculators and avocado pioneers like Edwin Hart had identified early on as prime for development. By the late 1950s, however, most of Vista's groves had died from root rot or had been removed for commercial development.

Meanwhile, avocado plantings in the subdistricts of the county's northern interior foothill areas climbed sharply. Despite the decline in Vista and Escondido, the county nearly doubled its avocado acreage between 1931 and 1947, rising from six thousand total acres to ten thousand, mostly in Fallbrook, Pala-Pauma Valley and Valley Center. By 1958, the county would have more than fifteen thousand acres, more than half the state's total.

Fallbrook

By 1960, one of these northern subdistricts, Fallbrook—a small, unincorporated town sixty miles north of San Diego—had quietly become the center of avocado production in California, earning it the nickname the "Avocado Capital of the World."

F.A. Lord planted Fallbrook's first grove in 1915, but production didn't take off until the 1940s, hitting thirteen thousand acres by 1963, the year of the town's first avocado festival. It would go through another surge in the 1970s, peaking in the late 1980s. Several subdistricts adjacent to Fallbrook—Rainbow and Valley Center, Pala and Pauma Valleys—absorbed the overflow, growing from thirty acres of avocados in 1950 to thousands of acres by 1970. Fallbrook became home to several packinghouses, mostly "independents" such as Del Rey, Pacificado, Eco Farms, Henry, McDaniel and Cal-Brook.

Fallbrook is ideally situated for avocados. It boasts an average yearly temperature of sixty-four degrees, with gentle topography, good soil, lots of sun and a low chance of frost damage. The town's population exploded between 1940 and 1960. In 1948, the *Fallbrook Enterprise* newspaper printed a letter from President Harry Truman thanking the people of Fallbrook for "the box of delicious Calavo avocados," which a contingent from the village had given him on his train trip through Southern California. A 1958 issue of *Look* magazine highlighted an avocado-themed dinner between famous Fallbrook residents Frank Capra and Duke Snider. Capra regaled the reporter with stories of how squirrels in his groves used avocados for "air-to-ground ballistic missiles." Other celebrities who have owned avocado groves include Rita Coolidge, Tom Selleck, Jamie Foxx and Jason Mraz. The town still holds its popular avocado festival, which is now in its thirty-seventh year.

In 1997, the state legislature officially renamed the twenty-two-mile stretch of I-15 between San Diego and the Riverside County line the "Avocado Highway." As a lawyer in 1989, Robert Jackson—the son of a Fallbrook physician and avocado farmer—played a key part in the renaming effort. (Jackson himself is now one of the area's largest avocado growers.) At its peak, the area contained nearly thirty thousand acres of avocados. Today, fewer than thirteen thousand acres remain.

In 1970, William Sterling Kerr III wrote a PhD dissertation for the University of Oklahoma on the "economic geography" of California avocados. In his analysis of the different "personalities" or regional attitudes of the three avocado regions, Kerr described San Diego County as "God's little one to four acres" (i.e., "ranchettes" on one- to four-acre lots with a single-family home). Kerr argued that, unlike most farmers—who pursue an agricultural occupation because it "provides them with a profitable livelihood"—the majority of San Diego growers "depend upon another occupation for primary support." These amateur farmers were an "over-

A program from the inaugural Fallbrook Avocado Festival in 1963. Today, more than seventy thousand people attend the event, which is held every spring in downtown Fallbrook. *Courtesy of SBC/THL.*

spill" from Los Angeles and urban areas of San Diego, attracted to rural settings near resort and recreation facilities. Avocado groves provided a "green milieu" with tax benefits, few neighbors and a more bucolic lifestyle. Even in 1969, Kerr concluded that this model of agriculture was "simply not economically feasible."

Kerr found that San Diego growers also tended to be "diverse, individualistic, and independent of spirit," as well as more affluent, educated and "inexperienced." This was a problem in the district, where "input costs" (water, labor, land, taxes and so on) are significantly higher than in the north. San Diego growers also relied heavily on professional grove managers, resulting in greatly reduced profits. This "independent spirit" also lessened Calavo's influence compared to the other counties. Several independent packinghouses existed in Fallbrook and Escondido, challenging Calavo's dominance. In 1966, disgruntled growers even formed a competing organization called the Avocado Growers' Council to challenge the newly formed industry marketing group.

In sharp contrast to San Diego, Kerr wrote that Ventura County was home to many large groves run mostly by professional farmers. Of 385 growers in the county, he found that 252 identified as full-time growers. Indeed, the majority were "longstanding professional farmers whose operation has been handed down through several generations." The more experienced, less affluent growers of Ventura, Santa Barbara and San Luis Obispo generally displayed "stable, well-organized, conservative farmer attitudes," compared to their colleagues in San Diego. There was little unrest among these "highly integrated farmers." Input costs also tended to be lower with more owners managing their groves.

Kerr's conclusion regarding the future of avocados in San Diego County was sobering. "If the avocado industry fails to overcome such problems as root rot, urbanization of avocado acreage, and labor problems," he wrote, "the last remaining stronghold of avocados in the United States is seriously threatened."

The divergent personalities of the two avocado districts have remained essentially consistent since 1970. If anything, the contrast between them has grown starker as economic pressures in the form of increased development, competition and water and labor costs began to roil San Diego farmers beginning in the late 1980s. This is discussed in more detail in the "Avocado Revolution" chapter.

A CRISIS OF CONFIDENCE

Since its founding, the avocado industry understood the vital importance of marketing. The founders who created Calavo in 1924 based the organization on Sunkist Growers, the wildly successful citrus marketing exchange company. Over a relatively short period, Sunkist had made oranges a staple food for Americans, shipping their products across the nation.

Although inexperienced and underfunded, Calavo and its directors followed Sunkist's blueprint for success. The exchange spent its marketing dollars on decorative fruit crate labels, postcards and retailer information sheets, recipe books, dietetic and nutritional pamphlets, radio spots, grocery store displays and ads in newspapers and magazines. It purchased several large packing plants in Escondido, Vista and Santa Paula, with modern mechanized equipment, oil-maturity testing laboratories, cooling facilities and sophisticated sizing and processing equipment. It also offered integrated grove care and management for members who did not want to tend their own groves.

Despite these accomplishments, Calavo still struggled to market an expensive exotic fruit to those outside the western United States.

In the mid-1950s, some growers began to resent the exchange's monopoly on marketing, which they felt had failed to open up the East Coast markets to their fruit. They also bristled at Calavo's heavy influence on fruit movement and prices. They expressed frustration at the inability of university researchers like George Zentmyer—whose work was largely funded by Calavo dues—to cure the root rot fungus plaguing the industry, even after twenty-five years. Angry growers began striking off on their own, joining independent packinghouses with their own marketing and distribution.

In 1958, heavy production led to a calamitous decline in avocado prices. From a high of $0.23 per pound in 1956, prices had tumbled to $0.05 by 1959. The disaster brought this crisis of confidence in Calavo to a breaking point. While most understood that aggressive marketing and education were necessary to expand this "unlimited" market, a vocal minority was beginning to think that Calavo was no longer the right organization to accomplish that goal. Some called for a new organization that would focus solely on the kind of modern marketing that would expand the borders of Avocado Land.

That change would finally take place in 1960 with the establishment of a marketing association that would become known as the California Avocado Commission.

The Story of Guacamole

Guacamole is a savory dish made from mashed avocados, often mixed with salt, citrus, onion, cilantro, sour cream, peppers, garlic or any combination

AVOCADO CRATE LABELS

In the late 1800s, a hungry nation discovered California citrus, which had been growing in the state for a century and was being shipped around the country on the newly built South Pacific and Santa Fe Railroads. To help their fruit survive the long journey, growers designed rectangular wooden crates to replace the baskets and barrels previously used. Around 1885, citrus growers started printing colorful paper labels, usually eleven by ten inches, to paste onto the ends or heads of the wooden crates. Over the years, the industry made more than eight thousand different fruit box labels.

In the 1930s, avocado growers and handlers began creating their own labels. The labels served the same purpose as those used for orange crates, advertising avocados shipped by Calavo, as well as by the many independent handlers such as Index, Henry Avocado, United Avocado Growers, Cal-Brook and others. Given the relative dearth of avocado handlers, especially in the first twenty-five years of the industry, fewer than one hundred different types of labels were produced before the industry transitioned to pre-printed cardboard boxes in the mid-1950s.

"I love the images," said Tom Spellman, one of only a few avocado label collectors. "They're from local towns and are very nostalgic. Almost all labels came from packinghouses that somehow kept them after they went to cardboard boxes. Back east, you can still find old crates with the labels on them." Spellman estimates that he has about fifty different avocado labels.

of these and other ingredients. Humans have probably enjoyed some version of the dish since the first peoples of the Americas discovered avocados thousands of years ago in what is now Latin America. The Aztecs of Central Mexico called the dish *ahuacamolli*, from the Nahuatl language meaning "avocado" (*ahuacatl*) "sauce" (*molli*). Sometime after the conquest in 1521, the Spanish altered the name to the modern spelling we use today. For Americans, if not for most of the world, guacamole is the most popular way to consume avocados. In fact, many have never eaten the fruit any other way.

The first recipes for guacamole in California didn't mention the original Spanish name. After all, even the name "avocado" was too exotic for some Americans. Instead, guacamole was usually referred to as avocado "dip," "spread" or "salad." In the seminal 1905 article for the USDA titled "The Avocado: A Salad Fruit from the Tropics," Guy Collins includes a recipe for

This 1949 Calavo advertising booklet marked the first time the company included a recipe for "avocado dip" using its original Spanish name—guacamole. *Courtesy of Calavo Growers.*

"avocado salad" from the *Cooking School Magazine* in which ripe "aguacates" are crushed together with diced tomatoes, green peppers, salt, onion juice and lemon juice or vinegar. West India Gardens reprinted the recipe in a 1913 advertising pamphlet.

Before the 1960s, the relatively few Americans who consumed avocados rarely ate them in mashed form. In the 1917 yearbook, Joseph Henry Pendleton, an avocado hobbyist and retired U.S. Marine Corps brigadier general (after whom Camp Pendleton is named), noted that the "favorite manner of eating the avocado among Americans is to cut the fruit in two lengthwise, removing the seed, and eating the pulp with a spoon." Pendleton lists six other ways to consume the fruit before finally mentioning what we would recognize as a sort of nondescript guacamole, which he describes as a "delicious puree made by mashing the pulp and using it as one would use green peas."

Even John Coit himself—the "Father of the California Avocado Industry"—was apparently not overly familiar with the dish. On a goodwill Society trip to Mexico in 1948, the hosts served Coit and his fellow industry leaders a "wonderful avocado dish known as 'Guacamole.'" Coit reported that "those of us unaccustomed to such a rich and highly flavored dish partook rather sparingly." In the 1950s, pioneering experiments by Calavo and others to create frozen, processed avocado usually referred to their product as "avocado dip" or "whip."

In the 1960s, guacamole rose in popularity thanks in large part to a massive influx of Mexican migrants and the subsequent proliferation of Mexican food restaurants. An explosion of snack foods (including tortilla chips) in supermarkets also drove the newfound fondness for the dip. In the late 1990s, with the passage of NAFTA and the importation of Mexican avocados, new advertising campaigns led by the California Avocado Commission, the Hass Avocado Board and other marketing associations promoted guacamole as the quintessential snack for Fourth of July festivities, Cinco de Mayo and Super Bowl parties.

Today, Americans spend more than $80 million on avocados and avocado products during Super Bowl week alone, consuming more than one hundred tons of the fruit. Since 2020, the Mexican avocado marketing association (Avocados from Mexico) has paid for multimillion-dollar ad spots for avocados during the big game on television and in retail stores. "Guac" was added to the Oxford English Dictionary in 2013.

....

Guacamole

From the Calavo Book of Popular Avocado Recipes, *1949*

In 1949, Calavo used the Spanish name for mashed avocados, guacamole, in an advertising pamphlet for the first time, complete with a helpful pronunciation guide ("wah-ka-mó-lay"). At the time, most would have used Fuerte avocados to make this recipe. However, the upstart Hass was already beginning to nip at Fuerte's heels by the 1950s. By the mid-1970s, Hass had replaced Fuerte as the industry's bellwether variety.

For a recent Super Bowl party, I brought two bowls of guacamole made using this seventy-five-year-old recipe. I made one bowl with Fuerte avocados from Atkins Nursery in Fallbrook. For the other, I used Hass avocados from Mexico. In a blind taste test of fifty acquaintances and friends, partygoers preferred the Fuerte version by a two-to-one margin. However, as anyone who regularly eats them knows, avocados can vary widely due to many factors. That's why the best avocados are usually those that are perfectly ripe and mature, regardless of type or country of origin. To my mind, however, it is nearly impossible to match the flavor of a fresh California avocado.

INGREDIENTS
1 medium-sized avocado
1 tablespoon lime or lemon juice
1 ½ tablespoons grated or minced onion
1 teaspoon salt or to taste

With a fork, combine ingredients but don't overmix.

AVOCADOS GO MAINSTREAM

1960-1980

Has the avocado advertising investment returned a profit to the grower? The answer is an emphatic yes!

—Ralph Pinkerton, 1963

From the postwar boom of the mid-1940s, the United States found itself in the throes of a rapidly expanding economy and population. Between 1960 and 2000, the U.S. population rose from 176 million to 250 million, with disposable income per capita more than doubling during that period. Beginning in the 1970s, the Hispanic population swelled, especially in California and the Southwest. In 1970, Hispanics numbered 10 million. Within a decade, there were 15 million, a 50 percent increase. Since the avocado is a staple of Latin American cuisine, more Hispanic consumers meant higher demand for avocados and thousands of new Mexican restaurants.

California's avocado plantings experienced three periods of expansion since the industry's founding in 1915. The first expansion occurred between 1920 and 1946, when the bearing acreage of avocados rose from 280 acres to 13,565 acres. The second took place a decade later, when a spate of intensive plantings in the early 1950s pushed total acreage well above 20,000 by the end of the decade. The result of this second expansion was the 140-million-pound crop of 1959–60, which sent prices crashing to a record low. In the 1970s, a third expansionary period began that would dwarf the previous two, both in terms of plantings and overall sales.

The industry understood that it had to mitigate the boom and bust cycles caused by the dramatic swings in price and volume. Most everyone agreed that the best way to accomplish this was to increase market demand; too few people were eating avocados, if they could find them in their stores at all. But this was easier said than done. For the industry's first forty years, the associations worked to develop the avocado market in the United States, drawing from a relatively meager budget funded by membership dues and periodic assessments. As a surge of new handlers began enticing growers away from Calavo, there was an urgent need to create a new industry-wide program of advertising and promotion apart from distribution.

A New Marketing Association

In 1959, the largest handlers formed a voluntary program called the California Avocado Development Organization (CADO). After CADO collapsed, a committee of growers and packers (including Calavo) petitioned the California Department of Food and Agriculture to issue an order that would allow for mandatory assessments for the sole purposes of avocado marketing. The order was issued in October 1959 and went into effect two years later, creating the California Avocado Advisory Board.

The new marketing order mandated grower assessments of gross annual sales of avocados to support board activities. The board took over all marketing duties previously performed by Calavo and some functions of the Society as well. In contrast to Calavo, the board did not sell fruit and had no say on how, when or where fruit was marketed or harvested. Instead, its principal task was advertising and promotion, along with public relations, trade and food service advertising, industry and government relations and research.

In 1978, the advisory board became the California Avocado Commission (CAC, or the Commission), which removed the state agency and gave local growers and handlers more control. Initially, CAC's board of directors was composed of ten commercial avocado growers from five newly defined districts, four handler representatives and a public member.

Given the demoralized and fractious nature of California's growers after the crash of 1959, the industry may have had low expectations of the Commission. However, as with Wilson Popenoe, George Hodgkins, John Coit and Jack Shepherd, CAC was fortunate in its selection of its first manager.

Ralph M. Pinkerton—or "Pink," as he was known to his friends—became CAC's first manager in 1960. A pianist and an aficionado of jazz music, fine dining and fancy cars, Pinkerton brought a touch of Hollywood to the mundane world of avocado marketing. His confidence, charisma and out-of-the-box thinking made an impression on all who worked with him. His marketing background in the much bigger and established apple industry taught him that promoting a relatively unknown fruit like the avocado was going to cost a lot of money. Within a year of becoming manager, Pinkerton convinced the board that the new grower assessment should be based on a percentage of crop sales rather than a set price of a few cents per box. The assessment was set at 5 percent of gross sales, although this percentage would fluctuate over the years.

As the first president of the California Avocado Advisory Board (later the California Avocado Commission), Ralph "Pink" Pinkerton revolutionized avocado marketing in the 1960s. *Courtesy of SBC/THL.*

By the mid-1960s, avocado production was growing at a fast pace. Increased sales meant more money for advertising and promotions. Soon enough, the Commission's successes were the envy of the entire fruit industry. In an address to the Society in 1967, Pinkerton observed that in the five years preceding the marketing order, the industry had sold 438 million pounds of California avocados for $42 million. Since the start of the advisory board in 1962, nearly the same amount had been marketed for $57 million, a 36 percent increase. Pinkerton attributed much of this to the Commission's efforts: "[T]here are definite indications that five years of advertising have been profitable for the California avocado industry.... The [Commission] knows that it must direct its advertising programs like a football coach runs his team. The consumer keeps developing new defenses to old advertising techniques and they must be shifted constantly, inventing fresh approaches, new plays to score with her."

Pinkerton and his staff knew that to win the marketing game, the industry had to grow per capita consumption in the large cities east of the Rocky Mountains. One study in the early 1960s indicated that only 5 percent of the U.S. population were consistent consumers of avocados. Most of these

Calavo's frozen avocado dip in 1964 became a huge seller for the company. *Courtesy of Calavo Growers.*

were in California, followed by several other western states. While the Commission did much to target states outside the West Coast, regular per capita consumption of avocados was only 1.5 pounds by 1976. Still, brand recognition was rising, as was per capita consumption in the western region.

Pinkerton's efforts were buoyed in 1964 when Calavo developed its first processed consumer product, a simplified version of guacamole dip. Initially, the dip came in refrigerated cans, but by the 1970s, a frozen version had become available in the same cardboard canisters used for juice concentrate. After some early struggles, Calavo ramped up marketing to the restaurant trade. The development of chips and the snack food industry also helped sales. Within a few decades, Calavo Foods was selling 20 million pounds of guacamole annually.

Although television became an effective vehicle for advertisers after 1976, Pinkerton and his successors at CAC felt that the targeted use of print ads was more cost effective. Point-of-sale promotions in grocery stores had always been an important means of advertising, but now most of CAC's budget went to printed advertisements in popular consumer magazines aimed at women, such as *Redbook, Ladies' Home Journal, Cosmopolitan, Vogue* and others. These publications offered recipes, nutrition information and food and lifestyle trends.

Pinkerton also maximized CAC's advertising dollars through his pioneering use of so-called tie-in advertising. He searched out compatible food marketers, persuading them to share the cost of magazine advertisements. Typical partners included established names like Kraft, Morton Salt, Frito Lay, Doritos, Pepsi, Sunkist, Betty Crocker and dozens

Left: A CAC promotion from 1979 cleverly links avocados to the finer things in life and capitalizes on the then-popular fad of growing an avocado in water from its seed. *Courtesy of SBC/THL.*

Opposite: Pinkerton's innovative use of "tie-in" advertising helped broaden the appeal (even the sex appeal!) of avocados. *Courtesy of SBC/THL.*

of others. Some tie-ins were no-brainers (chips, lemons, salad dressing, tequila, taco supplies and so on), while others seem more dubious (Jell-O, Rice-a-Roni, Almaden wine, tires, hash browns and cooking sherry).

"The Commission has been thought of as having a lot of marketing funds, but we really didn't," explained Jan DeLyser, an icon of the produce industry who served as a marketing executive at CAC between 1998 and 2023. "We had to be very careful how we spent those funds. We tried to figure out how to maximize the approach."

One unusual tie-in was for women's beauty products. In the early 1970s, the beauty industry decided that raw avocados were a useful ingredient in facial creams for women. As a result of this fad, CAC generated *The Fresh Avocado Beauty Book*, which was offered as a point-of-sale item in grocery stores and as part of tie-in campaigns with Revlon, Max Factor and other companies. Similarly, when "avocado green" became a fashionable color in the late 1960s and 1970s, CAC sought tie-ins with appliance companies. They even exploited the brief 1970s craze of growing your own avocado seedling from a pit suspended in a glass of water. In the late 1970s, CAC began a campaign aimed at the East Coast, advertising avocados as the "Love Food from California."

While not always successful, these efforts helped broaden the market appeal for avocados. Unfortunately, eastern markets remained a hard nut to crack for the Commission. By 1995, shipments to the eastern and southern regions of the United States had risen but still amounted to less than 26 percent. Most avocados stayed in California (39 percent) or went to Oregon, Washington or the Southwest (32 percent).

"Would This Body Lie to You?"

Perhaps Pinkerton's greatest marketing coup—one that would expose millions of Americans to California avocados like nothing before it—occurred in 1981. In its early years, the industry consistently heralded its

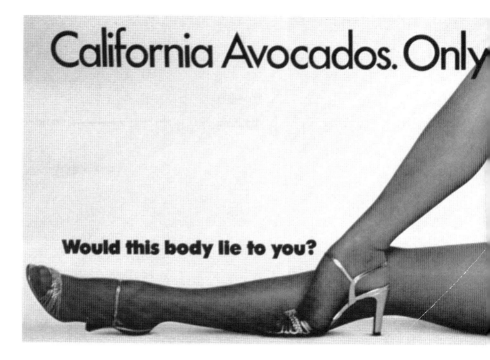

California Avocados. Only

Would this body lie to you?

California Avoca

For merchandisir

(east) Ron Hughes 714/540-8180; (midwest) Ron Set▮

4533-B MacArthur Blvd., Newport Beach, CA 92660   202 West Tower Drive, Tower L▮

product's nutritional value. In the early 1900s, the few researchers in the new field of nutrition science who actually studied the avocado praised it as an ideal, nutrient-dense food source. Of course, early advocates also routinely exaggerated the fruit's virtues. (The "Avocado Revolution" chapter discusses the topic of nutrition in detail.) In general, though, there seemed to be a consensus before 1960 that avocados were what many would later call a "superfood." In the 1960s, however, various entities began targeting avocados as a high-caloric, fatty food to avoid, challenging the fruit's nutritional bona fides.

An early example of anti-avocado fervor was the inclusion of the fruit on a list of "poison foods" in a 1966 copy of *Cosmopolitan* magazine. "Keep away

'calories a slice.

Angie Dickinson

do Commission

sistance, phone ────────────────
12/526-7835; (west) Bobbi Friedrich 602/839-3718.

arrington, IL 60010   1925 East Duke, Tempe, AZ 85283

A CAC advertising campaign starring Hollywood actor Angie Dickinson became one of the most famous advertisements of the 1980s. *Courtesy of SBC/THL.*

from them," advised columnist Joan Dunn in her dieting column. "They are high in calories and are destructively dangerous to you!" (In a 1966 letter to Calavo's lawyers, Shepherd asked whether he could sue the magazine for "irreparable injury and economic loss." They advised against it.)

As a result, CAC began to push the health angle more aggressively in its marketing, although the budget didn't allow for funding scientific studies. Eventually, the voices criticizing avocados on health grounds—combined with an avocado glut caused by the massive 1978–79 crop—began to erode sales. In response, Pinkerton and the Commission devised a provocative new ad campaign that addressed the fat issue head on.

The story goes that Pinkerton met television and movie star Angie Dickinson at a Hollywood party, and the two struck up a friendship. When he found out that she enjoyed avocados, he asked her if she would be in a new ad campaign for CAC. She agreed.

Over the course of a week, Dickinson shot a series of ads, both for print and television. In the television ad, a leggy Dickinson reclines casually on the floor in gold stilettos and a white leotard. As the camera pans slowly across her, she says, "This body needs good nutrition, including vitamins A, B1, C, potassium, niacin, iron, and this body gets them all in California avocados for just 153 calories in a luscious half shell." Continuing to gaze seductively at the camera, Dickinson gives a few helpful tips on how to ripen the fruit, concluding with what became one of the most memorable lines of any ad from the 1980s: "Would this body lie to you?"

The ad was a smashing success, generating the highest score ever measured by a Gallup Poll at the time. The Commission would run the spot for the next two years on television, in hundreds of magazines and on thousands of display posters in supermarkets across the country. While the war on the avocado continued, the tide had turned.

THE AVOCADO GOLD RUSH

Despite rising enthusiasm among the American public for California avocados, few in the industry anticipated the avocado "gold rush" that began in the 1970s.

Between 1970 and 1984, California saw an explosion in avocado plantings, both in the northern subdistricts of San Diego and in Ventura and Santa Barbara Counties. In 1974, there were 20,741 bearing avocado acres in the state. By 1984, that number had skyrocketed to 72,296. Crop production went from 100 million pounds in the mid-1970s to an average of 350 million pounds in the 1980s. Acreage finally peaked at 76,307 in 1988, before beginning a slow decline.

What caused this unprecedented surge in plantings? Much of it was due to the rising popularity of avocados, thanks in large part to the Commission's successful marketing. More demand for avocados meant more growers and more trees. Nurseries sold an average of 400,000 avocado trees annually between 1971 and 1975, mostly Hass. Meanwhile, the number of growers

HOW TO PREPARE AVOCADOS FOR EATING AND RECIPE USE

(You will be referred back to these basic directions in following the recipes in this book.)

IN ALL RECIPES, START WITH FULLY SOFT AVOCADOS, PLEASE, AND BRUSH ALL CUT SURFACES WITH LEMON OR LIME JUICE.

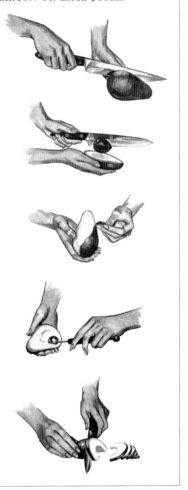

FOR HALF-SHELLS: Halve avocados lengthwise, twisting gently to separate halves. Whack a sharp knife directly into seeds and twist to lift out. You may use half-shells with or without skins.

TO PEEL HALF-SHELLS: Place cut-side down, in palm of hand. Strip or pare the skin. These half-shells may be cut into *quarters or eighths*.

FOR BALLS: Scoop out meat of *unpeeled* halves with melon cutter or ½ teaspoon measure.

FOR RINGS: Halve avocados crosswise. Whack out seeds and peel, then slice across.

FOR SLICES: Place *peeled* halves cut-side down to prevent breaking. Cut lengthwise or crosswise into crescents. Lengthwise slices may be *diced* or cut into *cubes*.

FOR ANGLED SLICES: Use *peeled* halves. Starting at narrow end, cut into thin slices on a sharp angle. This method displays both inside and outside avocado color and makes a pretty design for open sandwiches, salads and side dishes. Lay slices out in a line or in a fan shape.

FOR PURÉE: Mash *peeled* avocado with fork or force through sieve or food mill or purée in electric mixer or blender. Blend by portions when working with large amounts.

This advertising booklet from the mid-1970s includes a step-by-step guide on preparing avocados that is still helpful today. *Courtesy of SBC/THL.*

doubled, from 5,300 in 1970 to more than 8,000 by 1987. (Today, there are roughly 3,000 growers in the state.)

Another reason for this green gold rush had to do with taxes. Congress has long given farmers special tax rules to assuage the ups and downs of the agricultural cycle. In California, especially San Diego County, many high-income, nonprofessional or "gentlemen" farmers began to use these rules to reduce their tax burden by investing in agricultural operations. As discussed earlier, growers in San Diego County—as opposed to their counterparts to the north—were primarily interested in farming avocados as a secondary source of income or a post-retirement hobby. Beginning in 1970, doctors, attorneys, pilots, business executives and others discovered that they could save money in taxes by planting avocados.

"In my opinion, the avocado industry got started here in this part of the country because of high-cash income individuals," said Charley Wolk, a Fallbrook grove manager who has been a leader in the industry for more than fifty years. "Back then, there was an investment tax credit. It's not a deduction, it's a credit. So if you owe $20,000 in income tax, and you spend $20,000 developing an avocado grove, you subtract it from the $20,000 tax liability. The credit created the development."

More than ten thousand acres were planted in the county before the legislature closed the loophole in 1976.

INNOVATIONS

The steep and arid hillsides of San Diego, however, would not have been developable as groves had it not been for a pair of new inventions: drip irrigation using plastic hoses and the widespread availability of PVC piping.

Avocado trees are highly water dependent, especially in their youth. Before drip irrigation, growers watered their groves using flood irrigation or with fixed or rotating sprinklers. Besides being wasteful and expensive, these methods were simply not feasible for hillsides. In the 1950s, Simcha Blass pioneered drip irrigation using pressurized water through plastic hoses and emitters. Blass successfully used the system to irrigate crops at the Kibbutz Hatzerim in Israel. Beginning in the late 1960s, Don Gustafson—San Diego County's talented UC Cooperative Extension farm advisor—and others began a series of experiments using different types of irrigation systems. Gustafson found that with careful management, drip irrigation was an excellent solution to the high cost of imported water and hillside plantings.

This 1783 work by Ecuadoran painter Vincente Albán shows a sliced avocado on a table with other fruits from the Americas. *Courtesy of Los Angeles County Museum of Art.*

All avocado varieties are related to one or more of three original "races"—Mexican, Guatemalan or West Indian. The avocados shown here are mostly hybrids propagated in the twentieth century. *Courtesy of Julie Frink.*

36192
Early
Avocado
E. S. Rolfs
Miami
Dade Co. Fla.

A. A. Newton
Nov. 15, '11
After H. G. Passmore
7-15 '06

A drawing of the interior and exterior of an unknown avocado variety by Amanda Newton, 1906. *Courtesy of U.S. Department of Agriculture.*

A 1931 advertising pamphlet from Calavo Growers. Established in 1924, Calavo was the industry's first marketing exchange, representing most of the state's growers until the 1960s. *Courtesy of Calavo Growers.*

An artist's depiction from a 1943 postcard of avocado harvesting in San Diego County. *Author's collection.*

Opposite, top: Before the advent of pre-printed cardboard boxes in the 1950s, many handlers used avocado crate labels to advertise their fruit. *Courtesy of Tom Spellman.*

Opposite, second: Avocado crate label produced in the 1940s by Index Mutual Association, a cooperative exchange in La Habra. Now called Index Fresh, the company still ships fruit from its headquarters in Bloomington, California. *Courtesy of Tom Spellman.*

Opposite, third: Bob Elsinger opened one of the first packinghouses in Escondido in the 1920s and once owned groves throughout northern San Diego County. This label dates from the mid-1940s. *Courtesy of Tom Spellman.*

Opposite, bottom: Created in 1938, Bravocado is still a top brand for Henry Avocado, one of the state's oldest and most successful handlers. Founded in Escondido in 1925, Henry is still family-owned. *Courtesy of Tom Spellman.*

Above: Grower Ralph Foster at his house in Rainbow, California, with his avocado crate label collection behind him. Foster's father started one of the early independent packinghouses in Fallbrook. *Photo by Rob Crisell.*

Hass avocados nearing harvest at one of the organic groves owned by Eco Farms. *Courtesy of Eco Farms.*

UC–Riverside researcher Bob Bergh (*kneeling*) confers with avocado rancher Bob Lamb at Lamb's one-thousand-acre ranch in Camarillo in the 1980s. The work of Bergh and other UCR researchers resulted in many new varieties, including Gwen, Sir Prize, Harvest, Lamb Hass, GEM and Luna. *Courtesy of UC–Riverside.*

Makes youngsters feel like grownups and grownups feel like youngsters!

Pep up Pop ... and the whole family with Calavo avocados. This subtropical fruit with the delicate nutlike flavor contains amazing properties for the young and the young in heart ... 11 vitamins and 14 minerals ... linoleic acid for youthful vigor ... 100 to 150 calories in half an avocado.

Calavos are so easy to digest that pediatricians recommend them for infant and child feeding. There's nothing like an avocado. And there are no avocados like CALAVO brand. The CALAVO gold stamp means best varieties and proper maturity for finest eating quality.

For Spring Salads

A sure cure for spring fever is this tossed green salad with Calavos. Simply peel and slice, or dice a Calavo, and mix with fresh spring vegetables. Sprinkle lightly with lime juice, seasoned salt or your favorite dressing.

For Spring Lunches

Everyone loves Calavo hamburgers. Merely mash a Calavo, and season to taste. Try it "hot" with Tabasco sauce and chopped onions, or real cool with lime juice and seasoned salt. Spread on hamburger.

Free Growth Chart and Recipes

Calavo has a decorative, colored growth chart to record your child's development into teen-age. For this free Growth Chart and free Recipe Booklet, write Calavo, Dept. 46-B, Box 3486, Los Angeles 54.

Serve only when soft • Look for this quality stamp

CALAVO ᴮᴿᴬᴺᴰ AVOCADOS

LA 121—3/5 page, 4 colors—Sunday Supplement, March 25, 1956—3

A typical Calavo ad from the mid-1950s. Calavo spent most of its advertising budget on ads in women's lifestyle magazines. *Courtesy of Shepherd-Brokaw Collection at the Huntington Library.*

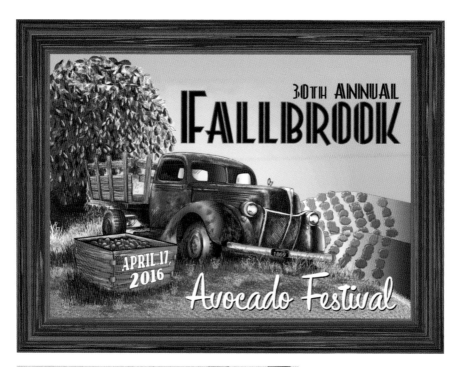

ALMADÉN AND AVOCADO.
FOR THE NIGHTS BEFORE CHRISTMAS.

How can you wrap up presents and wrap up parties too?
  Out in California we do it light and easy with our own Almadén
Wines and California Avocados.
  Luscious guacamole dip and smooth, satisfying avocado crescents
wrapped in ham.
  Both just right for the taking with aged-in-wood Almadén wine.
Like Johannisberg Riesling. A crisp, classic white. And Almadén
Ruby Cabernet. A full, bold red.
  So remember. Almadén Wine and California Avocado for all.
And for all a good night.

CALIFORNIA AVOCADO
ALA PROSCIUTTO.
Slice avocado into cres-
cents; ham slices
(prosciutto where
available) into strips.
Wrap, secure with picks,
drizzle with lemon
juice. Serves 8.

CALIFORNIA AVOCADO
GUACAMOLE DIP.
Lightly mash 4 avocados. Combine 1 tsp. seasoned salt, 2 Tbsp.
lemon or lime juice, 1/2 tsp. Worcestershire, 1/8 tsp. Tabasco, 1
finely chopped medium tomato.
Chill before serving with chips or
crackers.

Above: Since 1963, Fallbrook has celebrated its annual avocado festival. Fallbrook and the surrounding area once grew more avocados than anywhere else in the world. *Courtesy of Fallbrook Chamber of Commerce/Art by Kim Fiori.*

Left: One of California Avocado Commission's more unusual "tie-in" ads from 1975. *Author's collection.*

Top, left: Some California farmers plant GEM avocados because they can be grown in high-density plots. They are as gorgeous as they are delicious. *Courtesy of Organically Grown Company.*

Top, right: Jaime Serrato came to the United States from Mexico when he was ten. He has been a grower and grove manager for more than forty years. Behind him is Sam's Mountain Ranch, a 454-acre grove in Pauma Valley that Serrato planted in the 1980s. *Photo by Rob Crisell.*

Bottom: Luna is the newest hybrid to come out of Bob Bergh's breeding trials in the 1980s. Patented in 2023 by Mary Lu Arpaia and Eric Focht on behalf of UC–Riverside, the Hass-like Luna has a narrower tree structure that may enable high-density planting. *Courtesy of UCR / Photo by Stan Lim.*

Mini-sprinklers are extremely efficient and allow for a better distribution of water compared to ordinary drip irrigation. *Courtesy of Greg Alder.*

Inside Mission Produce's state-of-the-art facility in Oxnard. Once the biggest packinghouse in the world when it opened in 2015, Mission now owns even larger centers in Texas and Peru. *Courtesy of Mission Produce.*

Left: Avocado toast became a global phenomenon when it first appeared in restaurants in the 1990s. *Photo by Rob Crisell.*

Below: Recently grafted avocado trees in the greenhouse at Brokaw Nursery in Ventura County await transplant to larger pots. They will be grown for another year before delivery to commercial ranches around California. Brokaw is the largest producer of avocado trees in the United States. *Courtesy of Brokaw Nursery.*

Left: Here is the author's twist on the classic Caprese salad. For foodies, one of the best qualities of an avocado is its versatility. *Photo by Rob Crisell.*

Below: Overlooking the Brokaw avocado ranch in Santa Paula. In addition to its cutting-edge nursery, Rob Brokaw's farm is the site of ongoing horticultural experiments and innovation. *Courtesy of Brokaw Nursery.*

Above: A Mission Produce avocado farm on the campus of Cal Poly San Luis Obispo. *Courtesy of Mission Produce*.

Right: The author's mother, Toni Crisell, demonstrates her avocado picking skills in her Fuerte grove in Fallbrook, circa 1981. *Author's collection*.

West India Gardens and other nurseries often included avocado-themed recipes in their advertising, including a 1913 recipe for "Mexican Salad." *Photo by Rob Crisell.*

UC–Riverside researchers Mary Lu Arpaia (*right*) and Eric Focht (*left*) in front of a Luna tree, which the school patented in 2023. Arpaia has led UCR's avocado breeding program since 1997. *Courtesy of UCR / Photo by Stan Lim.*

Left: Guacamole in a traditional Mexican molcajete. Guacamole is derived from *āhuacamōlli*, the Nahuatl word for "avocado sauce." *Photo by Rob Crisell.*

Below: Historic Rancho Dos Pueblos ranch in Goleta. Simpatica purchased the ranch in 2015 and restored it to its former glory, farming four hundred acres of mainly avocados and cherimoya. *Courtesy of Simpatica/Photo by Scott Bauwens.*

Top: Avocado roses. *Courtesy of Collete Dike.*

Bottom: Avocado heart. *Courtesy of Collete Dike.*

Eventually, mini-sprinklers (developed initially by Rainbird) with larger distribution patterns replaced standard emitters. As drip irrigation took off, would-be avocado farmers snatched up formerly inaccessible land.

Funding New Research

Since its inception in 1915, the California Avocado Society supported research efforts related to the avocado. It accomplished this primarily by providing a forum in its meetings and journals, although a portion of its budget also went to direct funding. Most avocado studies in the yearbooks dealt with pests and plant disease, variety selection, soil studies, irrigation and cultural practices, such as frost avoidance, pruning, grafting, fertilization, production and cost control. Over the years, research categories expanded, along with their sophistication.

Most avocado research was conducted by a handful of California universities, including the University of Southern California, UC–Berkeley, UCLA, Cal State San Luis Obispo and particularly University California–Riverside, which evolved out of the Citrus Experiment Station in 1954. Avocado planting began at the Station in 1919 under the directorship of H.J. Webber. By 1970, nearly all avocado research was occurring at UC–Riverside or the South Coast Research and Extension Center in Irvine, California. Bob Bergh began the university's renowned avocado breeding program. Other well-known researchers at Riverside over the years include Bob Whitsell, John Menge, W.B. Storey, Gray Martin, Mary Lu Arpaia and Eric Focht. Plenty of other horticulturists—professional and amateur—contributed as well, like Julie Frink, Reuben Hofshi, Dennis Luby, Gregory Partida and many more.

In addition to on-campus academics, California Farm Advisors—a program formed by the State of California in 1913 and funded by the University of California, counties and the USDA—also played a vital role in research. Advisors provided (and still provide) direct and practical consultation with farmers, as well as conducted their own research projects as staff members of the University of California. Early farm advisors such as Marvin Rounds, George Goodall, James France, John Pehrson and Don Gustafson played crucial roles in grove development, acting as consultants to growers as well as liaisons between growers and the university. Other influential farm advisors included Gary Bender, Mary Bianchi, Ben Faber, Leonard Francis, Bud Lee and Guy Witney, among others.

In 1972, the Commission created a Production Research Committee, giving avocado research a much-needed boost. Between 1990 and 2000, CAC contracted with the Society to manage and sponsor research. Among other programs, the industry emphasized post-harvest research, such as transportation, processing activities and handling practices. In the 1990s, avocado-related studies began to taper off, although limited research continued, especially in the breeding program. Around 2015, the Commission finally ended its long-standing funding of that program and others.

Of the many UC–Riverside projects that the industry helped fund, the most ambitious was Dr. George Zentmyer's comprehensive research on root rot. Beginning in 1943, Zentmyer's thirty-five-year project led to the development of more resistant rootstocks, fungicides and better disease control and prevention. In the 1980s, Michael Coffey continued Zentmyer's research, with John Menge taking over from Coffey in 1990. Despite their efforts, root rot remains the most significant disease facing the industry.

UC–Riverside's Avocado Breeding Program

Since the late 1800s, amateur and professional avocado breeders such as Murrieta, Taft, Brokaw and the Popenoes sought to improve on the first avocado varieties from Mexico and Central America. Through trial and error, along with plenty of "avocado hunting" around Latin America, nurserymen and growers settled on Fuerte as the flagship variety. But Fuerte was far from an ideal fruit. It was often too sensitive to climatic conditions and was highly alternate bearing, meaning that trees produced robust crops only every other year. Other problems became evident over time, including skin blemishes, a sprawling tree structure and a susceptibility to smog. With the establishment of the UC–Riverside as a center for avocado research, CAC and the Society deemed it important to have scientists come up with a "better Fuerte"—one that would not only taste good and look good but would also bear more consistently.

Again, a person of genius emerged to answer the call. Berthold "Bob" Bergh was born in Canada, earning his doctorate in genetics at UC–Berkeley after serving in World War II. In the 1950s, Bergh began teaching at UC–Riverside. With funding from CAC and the Society, Bergh started the university's pioneering avocado breeding program, making him the first long-term breeder in history. Over a career spanning nearly five decades, Bergh developed a worldwide reputation as the leading authority on the avocado, helping countries like Israel, New Zealand and Kenya develop their own industries.

Bergh and his team set to work to develop a replacement for Fuerte. In the 1950s and early 1960s, some consumers were resisting the black-skinned Hass, which many associated with rotten fruit. In an effort to create a Fuerte-like avocado that would bear more consistently with a smaller tree size for easier harvesting and less pruning, Bergh planted thousands of genetically different seedlings of different varieties in volunteer and university-owned groves around the state. Eventually, he settled on Thille (an offspring of the Hass) as the best parent seedling.

In 1982, after two decades of work, Bergh and his colleague Bob Whitsell introduced the world to several avocados that had all the positive attributes of the Hass (excellent taste, thicker skin, summer harvest and a good shipper), with skin that stayed green even when ripe, like the Fuerte. "The University of California's avocado breeding program is reaching pay dirt," wrote Bergh in the 1982 yearbook introducing his three new varieties. Bergh named the most promising one "Gwen," after his beloved wife.

Unfortunately, Bergh's "pay dirt" turned out to be fool's gold. As Greg Alder—an avocado expert and blogger who wrote an update on the Gwen for the 2022 yearbook—put it, "Gwen really was dead on arrival." The problem was that by the time Bergh introduced his new hybrid, growers had planted tens of thousands of acres of Hass around the state. Moreover, thanks to CAC's marketing, Hass had overcome consumers' reservations about the color of its skin. Gwen was obsolete before it hit the market.

"We are now a 'Hass society,'" remarked Pinkerton at the 1982 Society meeting. "[We have] five times as many Hass this year as Fuertes, and over twice as many Hass as all of the other varieties put together….[I]t means we must plan our marketing around the major variety."

Despite this setback, neither Bergh nor the Commission was ready to abandon the breeding program. As good as it was, Hass still left room for improvement. Besides, many still hoped for a winter-spring avocado like Fuerte that might complement Hass's spring-summer season.

Bergh went back to work, planting seventy thousand Gwen offspring seedlings at three properties in San Bernardino, Ventura and San Luis Obispo Counties. Two of the sites proved to be failures, but the seedlings planted on fifteen acres of Bob Lamb's ranch in Camarillo proved to be the pay dirt that Bergh had been searching for with Gwen. (John Lamb and his family still farm more than three hundred acres of avocados on the ranch,

An in-store advertising display developed by United Avocado Growers, circa mid-1950s. UAG was one of the first handlers to market the new Hass variety. *Courtesy of Tom Spellman.*

which is part of Juan Camarillo's original 1876 Spanish land grant. John is Juan's great-great-grandson.)

With the help of his UC–Riverside colleagues, especially David Stottlemyer and a hardworking researcher named Gray E. Martin, Bergh's persistence resulted in several promising new varieties. After Bergh retired in 1991, the avocados he and his team invented were patented over the years as Sir Prize, Harvest, Lamb Hass and GEM. Of these, Lamb Hass and, more recently, GEM have made a small but significant impact on the California market. In 2023, UC–Riverside researchers Mary Lu Arpaia and Eric Focht successfully patented one of the newer hybrids—BL-516, which Martin had named "Marvel" in 1998—as "Luna UCR." The school partnered with Spanish horticulture company Eurosemillas to market Luna in Europe and the United States. *TIME* magazine named Luna as one of the best inventions of 2023.

A GEM of an Avocado

While Lamb Hass has been the most commercially significant avocado to come out of UC's breeding program to date—and Luna is the most recent—the GEM avocado may end up being one of the program's most commercially noteworthy legacies.

The GEM—named by and after its co-inventor **G**ray **E**. **M**artin—is a large, buttery ovoid variety with a pebbly green peel flecked with tiny golden specks. While slightly larger than the average Hass, GEM is like its older cousin in that it has thick skin, matures in spring and summer and turns black when fully ripened. In terms of eating quality, GEM and Hass are nearly indistinguishable; both have a rich, buttery texture and a smooth taste. One of GEM's advantages is that its "architecture" is much more compact and columnar than Hass, meaning that it can be planted more densely. Historically, twenty by twenty feet was the typical planting pattern for avocados. A more modern planting of Hass is fifteen by fifteen feet. By contrast, GEMs can be planted eight by fourteen feet or less—a 240 percent increase in trees per acre. GEMs also carry fruit inside their canopy, protecting them from sunburn and frost. As a bonus, the GEM scores high in blind taste tests and doesn't turn brown as quickly as Hass. No wonder then that some growers believe that GEM's advantages will ultimately lead the industry to jettison, or at least supplement, the Hass.

HASS DETHRONES FUERTE

As far back as the mid-1800s, California growers and botanists understood that the avocado possessed incredible variability, not just among its three races (Mexican, Guatemalan and West Indian) but among hybrids and offshoots of the same race. Since every seedling represents a potentially new variety, growers couldn't resist the urge to try to identify and propagate the perfect fruit.

Inventors of new varietals often shamelessly promoted their candidates, which they usually named after the fruit's birthplace or themselves (e.g., Taft, Anaheim, Puebla, Bacon, Dickinson and so on).

In 1926, postman and backyard grower Rudolph "Rudy" Hass of La Habra Heights planted a few Guatemalan seedlings he had purchased from the nearby A.R. Rideout nursery. The seedlings were Lyons, one of Rideout's proprietary varieties. Rudy and his neighbors soon grafted over their Lyon seedlings to Fuerte. While his graft worked on two of his trees, Rudy could not get the third tree to take on the Fuerte buds. After two more attempts, he gave up and allowed the tree to grow, although he ignored it.

In a year or two, the neglected tree began to bear fruit. Rudy thought that the avocado's black, pebbly skin looked unappetizing, so he made plans to remove it. However, his children had been eating the fruit and loved its rich buttery taste and texture. They urged him to try it before he cut down the tree. After the avocado won blue ribbons at a local fair, Rudy became a believer.

In 1935, Rudy Hass filed the paperwork to patent his new avocado, which was now thirty feet tall and bearing prolifically. Naturally, he named the variety after himself. (Hass rhymes with "pass," although most of the world pronounces it as "hoss.") He entered into a contract with pioneering nurseryman Harold Brokaw to graft the new Hass seedlings and market them to growers.

Unfortunately for Rudy and Brokaw, market acceptance of the dark-skinned variety was sluggish. Calavo had spent several decades and millions of dollars educating retailers and consumers to view green-skin avocados as the ideal. Consumers spurned dark-skinned "warty" varieties like Hass. Retailers also didn't appreciate that Hass competed with dozens

Rudy Hass with his wife, Elizabeth, in front of an avocado tree in La Habra Heights. In 1935, Rudy patented what would become the world's most popular avocado. *Courtesy of the California Avocado Commission.*

of other summer fruits. Stores would reluctantly purchase the variety during the summer months, but only at deep discounts. Hass didn't even crack Calavo's top ten heaviest volume varieties until 1950.

Not long after Rudy's passing in 1952, people began to warm up to his namesake variety. Calavo and CAC launched marketing campaigns to educate the public about the "black gems," an early nickname for Hass. Thanks to Hass's inherent advantages over Fuerte—higher and more consistent yields, more compact tree size, better shipping qualities—growers and handlers started demanding it. By 1957, Hass represented only 15 percent of the state's crop. Seven years later, it rose to 23 percent. In 1972, Hass finally surpassed Fuerte in market share, forty years after its introduction. As a result, peak avocado season shifted accordingly, from winter/spring to spring/summer.

By 1987, Hass accounted for 78 percent of California's total crop. King Fuerte had been deposed at last, tumbling to a distant second with only 8 percent of that year's total crop. Today, Hass represents roughly 95 percent of all avocados consumed in the United States and about 80 percent of all avocados worldwide.

Trials conducted at five sites by Arpaia compared Hass and GEM yields over a four- to seven-year period. (Brokaw Nursery conducted an additional trial.) Averaged across all six location and years, GEM trees yielded 55 percent more fruit compared to Hass. In those same trials, GEM fruit averaged 8.3 ounces, while Hass fruit averaged 7.1 ounces. Finally, GEM trees are much less alternate bearing than Hass, providing more consistent crops.

Most handlers remain skeptical about the GEM. Hass is already an excellent avocado with buy-in around the world, they argue. Why mess with a good thing? GEM growers counter that Hass, with its smaller yields and lower planting density, is no longer economically feasible in California, especially in light of astronomical water rates in San Diego County. Besides, they argue, consumers might appreciate a little avocado diversity in their grocery stores.

Arpaia is a firm believer in the importance of further avocado research. "Back in the 1920s when Henry Ford came out with the Model T, that car was revolutionary," she says. "But we're not driving Model T Fords anymore. We're driving these super smart cars. That's because people saw that you could still improve it. That's the name of the game in avocado breeding."

Since the one constant in Avocado Land is change, it should not come as a surprise to anyone if GEM, Luna or some unknown varietal one day challenges Hass for supermarket supremacy.

CHALLENGES AHEAD

By the end of the 1980s, the avocado industry appeared to be on the cusp of a new wave of expansion, thanks to big-budget marketing efforts, daring researchers, thousands of acres planted in a new productive varietal and innovations in irrigation, packing and shipping. However, road bumps lay ahead.

Even in sunny California, nature continued to wreak its usual havoc with avocados. In 1969, a crippling freeze killed nearly 90 percent of the crop in San Diego County. In 1990, one of the worst freezes in state history caused massive fruit losses and tree death, especially in Ventura County. Powerful Santa Ana winds in 1967 resulted in the loss of 1 million pounds of fruit in Pauma Valley. While the frequency of dangerous freezes would diminish over the coming years, the risk of wildfires would climb, due to high winds, larger populations in high-risk areas, droughts and warmer temperatures in Southern California. In 1984, the Grimes fire in Ventura burned 11,000 acres, including dozens of groves. In 2002, the Gavilan fire in Fallbrook destroyed hundreds of acres. Another Fallbrook fire in 2007 would do significant damage as well. In 2017, the Thomas fire in Ventura proved to be one of the most destructive in state history, burning 280,000 acres, including 6,600 acres of avocado groves.

The ravages of root rot disease began to lessen due in part to better grove management, as well as Brokaw Nursery's development of clonal root stocks that were more resistant to disease. Improvements in farming helped as well. Growers began to plant young trees in raised beds and were more careful about not spreading root rot from one tree to another. Treating groves with phosphonate fungistats helped trees tolerate, resist or recover from infection.

Meanwhile, after decades of expansion leading up to World War II, the rate at which new residents moved to California stabilized at between 1 percent and 3 percent for the next fifty years. However, the rate for San Diego County remained high, about 4 percent through 1990. The population of the county went from 844,000 (1960) to 1.8 million (1980) to 2.6 million (2000). This rapid urbanization caused a surge in land prices, taxes and fees. Since the 1960s, industry leaders like Charley Wolk and Mike Sanders of Fallbrook, Leonard Francis (farm advisor in Riverside), San Diego farm advisors Gustafson and Gary Bender (after 1985) and others had been warning that "input costs" were increasing, including water, land, labor, taxes and fees, fertilizer and pest and disease control. Farming was slowly becoming economically unfeasible for small farmers, who made up the vast majority of growers.

Finally, the sudden appearance of Mexico in the late 1990s as a dominant player in what had suddenly become an international, multibillion-dollar business represented the biggest challenge the industry had ever faced. The entrance of Mexican fruit into American markets would hurl California's growers into an existential crisis, forever transforming how Americans—and the world—would think about avocados.

....

Prosciutto-Wrapped Avocado Slices with Melon Sauce
From an industry sponsored "tie-in" with Almaden wine, 1975

One of CAC's contributions to the industry was pioneering the use of "tie-in" advertisements with established companies like Kraft, Frito Lay, Hormel and others. Variations of this recipe for prosciutto-wrapped avocado slices appeared in many different tie-in ads in the 1970s, including one with Almaden wines, a large wine manufacturer in San Joaquin Valley. While Almaden recommends its Johannisberg Riesling or Ruby Cabernet in the ad, I would suggest instead pairing this dish with a Napa Valley Sauvignon Blanc or a delicate Pinot Noir from Santa Barbara or Sonoma. I have taken the liberty of "elevating" the original recipe with an optional melon dressing and a drizzle of olive oil.

INGREDIENTS
¼ honeydew or cantaloupe melon (2 slices without rind)
2 tablespoons aged balsamic vinegar
4 ounces (16 thin slices) prosciutto
2 ripe avocados
Salt and pepper to taste

Puree the melon and vinegar in a blender or food processor until completely smooth. Gently wrap a slice of prosciutto around each avocado wedge and lay on a platter or individual plates. Drizzle the melon sauce over the wrapped avocado wedges and serve immediately.

AVOCADO LAND BECOMES AVOCADO WORLD

1980–2000

My point today is that for the future, Mexican avocados could be a problem only if you, as an industry, fail to recognize them as an opportunity.
—Ramon Paz-Vega, 1989

In 1967, Don Gustafson joined a group of California avocado growers and scholars on a trip to Mexico for a two-week study tour. Like similar trips in 1929, 1938 and 1948, the purpose was to meet with Mexican growers, observing and evaluating the country's avocado culture. It was a goodwill mission, replete with gratitude and mutual respect on both sides. Gustafson—San Diego County's farm advisor from 1953 to 1983 and a tireless UC Cooperative Extension researcher—was the driving force behind the use of drip irrigation and mini-sprinklers in California and one of the Society's most prolific authors.

The relationship between California growers and their counterparts in Mexico had long been an amicable comradeship of "avocadoistas." Americans regularly visited the avocado "Motherland" of Mexico, providing encouragement and expertise to growers in Puebla, Michoacán, Jalisco and other Mexican states. Of course, Mexicans had been going north for many years to learn valuable new techniques and knowledge from Californians.

Even in the 1960s, Mexico still did not pose much of a threat to the dominance of California avocados. The eighty-three-year-old quarantine on the importation of avocados was still in place, ostensibly because of the seed weevil, an aggressive pest that afflicted some of the country's groves. For most of the twentieth century, the ban had been a non-issue for Mexican growers. The country's commercial avocado industry had always been primitive, with relatively few packinghouses or commercial farms. Moreover, Mexicans were voracious consumers of avocados, with per capita consumption dwarfing that of Americans. In the 1960s, the average Mexican citizen was eating more than fifteen pounds annually, compared to just one or two pounds for the average American. What grew in Mexico stayed in Mexico.

When he returned to California, Gustafson shared his observations with CAS members at their annual meeting:

> *There is a great rush of planting grafted avocado trees. Avocado culture is relatively inexpensive. Water is abundant, convenient, and of good quality. The trees are being grafted to known varieties from California.… The Mexican is becoming more conscious of the profitability of growing avocados and this is why so many are going into the commercial growing and marketing of avocados.*

Nevertheless, Gustafson felt that Mexico's nascent industry still represented little threat to California in the near future.

In 1970, Gustafson and a few dozen CAS members—including Oliver Atkins, the pioneering nurseryman and grower from Fallbrook—returned to Mexico on a follow-up trip. Gustafson marveled at how quickly the country's avocado industry had changed in the intervening three years. Plantings had skyrocketed, especially in Michoacán, which was now the epicenter of avocado cultivation in the country. There were several new packinghouses and numerous commercial farms on an estimated forty-five thousand total acres. Yearly output was now roughly 440 million pounds, which matched or exceeded California's average production. New associations were working with academic institutions on avocado-related topics, including improvements in fertilization and pest control. Moreover, Mexico's input costs remained low. Labor was cheap, and the country's climate, varying geography and abundance of rainfall allowed for the continual harvesting of avocados throughout the year. As longtime CAS board member Leonard Francis later put it, "The Creator of the world did make several areas of Mexico ideal for avocados."

All this begged the obvious question: How long would Mexico be content to keep its avocados within its own borders?

How California Created Avocado World

Mexico's suddenly vibrant avocado industry—along with similar "startups" in a dozen other countries around the globe—happened as a direct result of decades of cooperation and support by the California Avocado Society and its members.

CAS is the oldest continually operating association of avocado growers in the world. Since its founding in 1915, the Society has documented, facilitated and celebrated the spread of avocado agriculture, not just in California, but everywhere else too. As one of the principal architects of the world's first industry, the Society has always embraced its role as avocado ambassador to the world. Long before Mexico emerged to challenge California's undisputed claim as Avocado Land, it was merely one of several countries struggling to cultivate the green fruit on a commercial scale. As these burgeoning industries arose, the Society regularly invited foreign scholars and cultivators to join its ranks to take advantage of the decades of collective knowledge and innovation.

The Society's yearbooks consistently highlight avocado developments abroad and the work of their members in those countries. In 1930, the yearbook included reports on avocado cultivation in India, Honduras, Australia and Israel. In 1936 and 1940, it published the first reports from Chile, Brazil, Algeria, Egypt, Italy, South Africa and Argentina. In 1934 and 1947, there were mentions of unlikely avocado plantings in southern Russia (then the USSR), where John Coit had sent sixty-three trees from Vista, California. Of course, the yearbook regularly included topics related to Latin America.

But Society members did more than publish speeches and articles. They visited countries as well, advising them and supplying them with grafted plant material, production research and other technology. As countries formed their own industries in the 1950s, they often enlisted Californians as advisors, including Wilson Popenoe in Honduras and Guatemala; C.A. Schroeder in Latin America, New Zealand, Africa and Southeast Asia; George Zentmyer in Australia and Latin America; Bob Bergh in Israel; Don Gustafson in Israel, South Africa and Mexico; Rob Brokaw in Spain; and Ben Faber in New Zealand and Turkey, among many others. In the 1950s, Mexican officials hired independent handler Gil Henry to advise growers in Michoacán. In the 1970s and 1980s, executives with Calavo, Mission Produce, Del Rey, Eco Farms, West Pak, Index and others assisted commercial growers in Latin America and elsewhere with their exports. Today, several California

AVOCADO PLANTING IN RUSSIA

Mr. A. J. Fomin of the Psyrzha State Farm at Abhasin, U. S. S. R., giving directions and planting the variety collection comprising 63 avocado trees from Southern California. The trees were packed and shipped from Vista January 15, 1934, by Dr. J. Eliot Coit. They arrived at their destination in good condition on March 12 and were planted immediately.

Avocado planting in the former USSR (possibly Georgia) in 1934. CAS helped numerous countries develop their own avocado industries. *Courtesy of California Avocado Society.*

handlers and larger growers own groves or packinghouses in Peru, Spain, Brazil, Chile, Mexico and elsewhere.

At the Society's seventy-second meeting in 1988, Salvador Sanchez Colin—a CAS director-at-large and a former director of agriculture for the Mexican government—lauded the Society and its members for their work in transforming Avocado Land into the "World of Avocados." As he put it, "An Australian, an Israeli, a Dominican, or a Mexican—all of us are pieces of the world's avocado agroindustry."

As Colin would have acknowledged, Mexico was the largest beneficiary of California's "avocado evangelism," thanks to its proximity, cultural ties and the length of the relationship. The benefits were mutual. Mexico supplied California with many of the state's early varieties (including Fuerte), most of the labor, a popular cuisine and immigrants who heavily utilized the fruit. At the same time, Mexico profited from California's many years of marketing, scientific research and technology. And it was a Californian, after all—Rudy Hass in 1935—who invented the eponymous variety that would eventually represent 95 percent of Mexico's plantings.

However, California's greatest contribution to Mexico's industry was the development of the most lucrative avocado market in the world: the United States of America.

Mexican Avocados Arrive at Last

While the Society is justifiably proud of its role in assisting Mexico and other countries with developing their industries, foreign avocados meant foreign competition.

Until the second half of the twentieth century, the only country with an avocado industry besides the United States was Cuba, which began routinely exporting significant numbers of avocados to the mainland in the 1930s. When Cuban exports were banned in 1959, California faced no significant foreign competition for another thirty-five years. Between 1962 and 1989, imported avocados to America amounted to just over 1 percent of annual U.S. production.

But the absence of foreign avocados in U.S. markets did not mean that other countries weren't growing them. In the 1960s, demand was rising quickly around the world, especially in the United States. This led to planting booms in California but also Mexico, Israel, Africa, the Philippines, Spain and throughout Latin America. In 1976, though, California's average avocado production still exceeded all other nations except Mexico, which was now approaching 600 million pounds per year.

By 1986, despite a furious spate of plantings in the late 1970s, California had lost more ground against its biggest competitor. At 400 million pounds, the state was now a distant second to Mexico, which hit a staggering 1.4 billion pounds, sourced from more than 200,000 acres. Brazil's output now stood at 600 million pounds, with the Dominican Republic and Israel hovering around 200 million. Ten other countries were catching up to the United States in terms of volume, but only the Dominican Republic and Chile were shipping avocados to the United States, usually in relatively small quantities and burdened with tariffs. Meanwhile, Mexico had begun shipping to Europe and Japan.

In the mid-1980s, the first cracks in the 1914 avocado quarantine began to appear. Several neoliberal free trade movements were sweeping through North American and European governments. With President Ronald Reagan's support, Congress authorized negotiations to institute a bilateral free trade agreement between Canada and the United States in 1984. On January 2, 1988, the two countries completed the United States–Canada Free Trade Agreement. As the agreement was being finalized, Mexico's President Salinas de Gortari—a free trade advocate and an economist with a degree from Harvard University—declared that his country wanted to join.

California's avocado industry—through CAC and Mark Affleck, the dynamic vice-president of industry affairs who would soon take over as president of the Commission—sounded the alarm. Affleck's 1986 address to the Society articulated the position of the vast majority of its members:

> *Of all the developing countries that have sought a free trade area with the United States, Mexico poses perhaps the greatest threat of all to the California avocado industry. Under no circumstances, free trade area or otherwise, should the integrity of this quarantine be jeopardized. To do so would risk contamination of our entire U.S. production. It is also quite evident that a relaxation of this restriction would subject our industry to an onslaught of additional avocado imports that we are ill-suited to accommodate....Free trade is OK, but it must be fair trade.*

Over the next few years, the United States, Canada and Mexico hammered out the North American Free Trade Agreement (NAFTA), which proposed to eliminate tariffs and other trade barriers between the countries, including the 13.2 cents per kilogram levied on imported avocados. In 1992, President Clinton signed NAFTA into law, superseding the United States–Canada Free Trade Agreement. In 2020, the United States–Mexico–Canada Agreement (USMCA) replaced NAFTA, maintaining and updating most of its predecessor's provisions.

In the decade following the ratification of NAFTA, California avocado growers—through the Society, CAC and other organizations like the Farm Bureau (headed up by Fallbrook nurseryman and grower Bob Vice)—engaged in ferocious lobbying with the USDA to mitigate what they saw as a potential disaster for the industry. One of the major concerns was making sure that the USDA had "phytosanitary" measures in place at Mexican packinghouses and at entry points into the United States to prevent diseases and pests from harming California's groves. Few disputed the need for such safeguards. The

STOP MEXICAN AVOCADO PESTS!

SHOW US THE SCIENCE!

Free trade YES! Free pests NO!

Sign from the late 1990s protesting the importation of Mexican avocados to the United States. *Courtesy of Scott Van Der Kar.*

other concern—sometimes unstated, though more salient—was to minimize the economic damage that a flood of cheap Mexican avocados might do to the state's industry.

For the most part, California's packinghouses welcomed the arrival of Mexican fruit. Handlers like Mission Produce, Calavo, Eco Farms, Henry, West Pak and Del Rey realized that American demand for avocados had already outpaced the state's supply. California's acreage was also in decline, from 76,307 bearing acres in 1987 to 61,254 in 1994. Only Mexico could guarantee Americans with year-round avocados. It helped that the Mexican industry planned to use American handlers for processing and distribution within the United States.

Drawing on their long relationship with California organizations like CAS, Mexican growers tried to allay the fears of their northern peers. At the 1989 Society meeting, Ramon Paz-Vega—then the chairman of the Union of Avocado Growers of Michoacán—told Society members that California growers should view Mexican avocados as "supplementing" the state's production, not replacing it. He also called opposition to Mexican imports as "more emotional than rational." "Why not change the threat into an opportunity?" he asked. "Everybody would benefit and competition would not increase."

In 1998, the first year of NAFTA, only 6.5 million pounds of avocados arrived in the Northeast from Mexico, per the provisions of the agreement. The following year, Mexico received access to twelve more states, as well as a longer import window. Exports rose to 20 million pounds and remained there for two more years. As late as 2000, California fruit still represented 75 percent of all avocado sales. However, this was about to change in a big way.

In 2001, Mexico pointed out that it had been nearly five years without the detection of insect pests or any other phytosanitary problems. It accused the USDA of acting unreasonably by not allowing unfettered imports as permitted under NAFTA. As a result of these negotiations, Mexican imports more than doubled to 48 million pounds the following year. In 2007, the federal government eliminated all import restrictions, allowing Mexico to ship as many avocados anywhere in the United States at any time. California's share of total domestic sales quickly plummeted from 60 percent to 30 percent, as Mexico sent more than 600 million pounds across the border, surpassing Chile as the largest importer.

But Mexico was just warming up. By 2018, the country was shipping more than 940,000 tons or roughly 1.8 billion pounds of fruit to the United States every year. Total avocado acreage in Michoacán now stood at 400,000 acres, with another 65,000 in Jalisco. By then, California's plantings had fallen to around 50,000 total acres. As of 2022, California's share of U.S. avocado sales hovered at around 7 percent, with an average of 250 million pounds or less produced between 2021 and 2024.

Ultimately, California won a number of battles that delayed the arrival of Mexico's avocados to the United States. It also instituted meaningful phytosanitary oversight over Mexico's industry, which remains in place today. However, the state had no chance of winning the war. The problem facing the industry was that avocados were—and are—a mere sliver of the U.S.–Mexico trade relationship. The value of imported Mexican avocados in 2021–22 amounted to less than half of 1 percent of total trade revenue between the two countries.

Still, Ramon Paz-Vega turned out to be correct. The flood of Mexican avocados did not destroy California's avocado industry, nor did it greatly lower the value of the state's fruit. Instead, it grew American demand for avocados by about 10 percent annually, or roughly 300 percent since the passage of NAFTA. Per capita consumption in the United States rose from two pounds to nine pounds, a level no one could have imagined before 1997.

Calavo versus Independent Packinghouses

Since the beginning, California's avocado growers took the lead in funding and directing the industry and its associations. In 1915, nearly all the Society's charter members were growers or horticulturists of one stripe or another. Yet the industry had also depended on other "students of the avocado," as an early founder phrased it, for its success. These included scientists, nutritionists, real estate developers, chefs, retailers, advertising executives and avocado obsessives. Over the years, one of these non-grower groups—independent avocado packinghouses or "handlers"—took on a much more central role.

In 1924, the Society hired George Hodgkin as the first manager of the newly formed California Avocado Exchange (later renamed Calavo Growers) to market and distribute its members' fruit. Calavo knew that it had to provide valuable services beyond what the ordinary grower could do by himself. If not, growers would continue to take their fruit directly to local markets themselves, lowering prices and endangering the entire industry.

Processing, shipping, marketing and selling growers' fruit—these services would remain largely the same over the next century, even as the industry continued to innovate and evolve. However, Calavo's principal role—as was true for independent handlers as well—was the effective shipping and marketing of avocados.

In 1955, Calavo built a new packinghouse in Santa Paula, which became the world's largest and most advanced facility. By the 1960s, Calavo had twenty-six sales offices in major cities around the United States and was distributing about 80 percent of the state's avocados. For Calavo to fetch top dollar for its growers' fruit, its directors knew it had to control how and when that fruit entered the market. That is why industry leaders did their best to discourage the use of independent handlers.

Despite this, independents continued to proliferate. According to William Kerr, Calavo still claimed 2,800 of California's 5,300 growers in 1968, but it was losing growers every day. By the 1970s, some independents had become

Calavo promotional signs at a grocery store in 1955. *Courtesy of SBC/THL.*

as vertically integrated as the venerable exchange, doing everything from packing, ripening, marketing and shipping to maintaining client's groves. Kerr noted that most of these handlers were "small in size with limited operating expenses and a few highly paid administrators."

Henry Avocado Company in Escondido is among the most successful of these original independents. Founded in 1925, it is still family owned and a major player in the industry, with distribution centers in California, Arizona, North Carolina and Texas. In his address to the Society in 1962, Warren Henry—who took over the company from his parents in 1953 with his brother Gil—laid out a few of the advantages of working with an independent handler:

> *Independent packers must compete on two sides. He must first compete for the grower's fruit, and secondly he must compete on the open market to distribute the fruit he has already purchased. His mistakes cannot be charged back to the grower as can those of a co-op manager....In the case of a co-op, of course, the growers share equally with other members in any such loss.*

By the 1980s, Calavo was losing many of its growers to independent packinghouses, which were located mostly in San Diego and Riverside Counties. In 1995, Avi Crane's report in the CAS yearbook stated that there were thirteen major handlers in California, although another fifty or so handled "minimal volumes." Of the thirteen, two controlled roughly 49 percent of the market, while another six controlled 27 percent.

As foreign avocados flowed into the United States from Chile, Peru and Mexico in the 1990s and 2000s, handlers went from processing millions of pounds of California avocados to processing billions of pounds of foreign avocados. Today, there are still roughly a dozen packinghouses handling more than 3 billion pounds of avocados annually, nearly all of it from Mexico. These include Henry (Escondido), McDaniel (Fallbrook), Del Rey (Fallbrook), Eco Farms (Temecula), Giumarra (Escondido), Mission Produce (Oxnard), West Pak (Temecula), Index (Bloomington) and others. In 2002, Calavo's members finally voted to take the company public after seventy-eight years as a grower cooperative. The state's largest handler, Mission Produce, followed in 2020 under founder and CEO Steve Barnard.

THE PRE-RIPENING REVOLUTION

Besides their role in marketing and distribution, handlers have long been catalysts for innovation within the industry. Examples include the adoption of mechanization (forklifts, hoists, pallet jacks), palletization and bins, new sizing and sorting machinery, drip irrigation, mini-sprinklers, fertilizers, clonal root stocks, varietal research and more. One of these innovations led to the industry's "pre-ripening revolution."

In the 1980s, the supply of California avocados exploded thanks to a surge of avocado plantings in the 1970s. Yet demand lagged behind, evidenced by low returns to growers. From 1974 through 1980, California's average crop size was 182 million pounds, with an average return of $0.39 per pound. Between 1981 and 1987, the crop ballooned to 422 million pounds, while the average return fell to $0.25 per pound.

As the industry searched for ways to convince Americans to consume more avocados, one issue kept cropping up in surveys: buyers were frustrated at not being able to find ripe avocados at the store. Usually, shoppers—as well as institutional buyers such as restaurants—had to "make a date" with their avocados rather than being able to use them the same day or soon after. Market research showed that countless sales were lost due to the absence of ripe fruit. In the CAS 1982 yearbook, an article by S.K. Lee and C.W. Coggins reported on their trials at Alpha Beta supermarkets demonstrating that soft avocados were significantly more desirable to consumers than non-ripe fruit. The Commission's study showed that retailers would get more than a 25 percent boost in sales if they offered ripe fruit.

Avocados mature on the tree, but they do not soften to ripeness there. Once picked, they generally need between seven to ten days at room temperature before they are ready to eat. To delay the ripening period, handlers cool down the avocados at the packinghouse before shipping them in refrigerated trucks. Prior to the invention of pre-ripening, retailers put green, hard fruit on display right away; there was no room to store them for any length of time. This meant that avocados would be inedible for a week or more. It also meant uncontrolled ripening en masse, leading to widespread "shrink"— that is, the spoilage of fruit before sale. Shrink caused retailers to order less fruit than they might otherwise to avoid wasting money.

Researchers conducted experiments in "pre-conditioning" or "pre-ripening" of avocados as early as 1941. They showed that avocados ripened with exposure to ethylene, a hydrocarbon gas that the fruit produces naturally once removed from the tree. In 1982, Victor Tokar—an Orange County

Modern ripening rooms at a Mission Produce facility. *Courtesy of Mission Produce.*

native and consultant for the produce industry—started experimenting on his own. He found that while ethylene did accelerate ripening, the carbon dioxide and heat generated did not dissipate well, harming the fruit.

"It did not take very long to realize that the air had to be physically moved through the carton's vent holes to remove this heat," wrote Tokar in 2008. "Both these obstacles, heat and excessive carbon dioxide, were solved by forcing air through the avocado pallet with a suitably sized fan and continuously venting the ripening room to the outside with a small fan."

In 1983, Tokar approached Gil Henry at Henry Avocado Company in Escondido to see if he would be willing to convert one of his cooling refrigerators into a small pre-ripening room. Henry embraced the idea, since he and the industry were facing a monstrously large crop that year. Henry reached out to Mike Aiton, director of produce at King Soopers in Denver. Aiton agreed to receive the pre-ripened fruit as an experiment. "Every chain store manager knows that their customers buy more avocados if they're ripe," said Henry in his personal account for the CAS 1985 yearbook.

At the packinghouse in Escondido, Tokar took recently harvested avocados and kept them at sixty-eight degrees for twenty-four hours. Then he added a small amount of ethylene gas for another twenty-four hours, venting as necessary. After the process was complete, Henry sent the avocados in standard refrigerated trucks to the grocery store. Once the retailer brought the fruit back to room temperature, it would be ready to eat within forty-eight hours.

When Aiton received Henry's fruit, he displayed the pre-ripened avocados alongside unripened fruit. To his delight, the ripe fruit sold at a rate of twenty-five to one over the hard fruit. He immediately ordered pre-ripened fruit for all sixty-three stores around the state. Within a few months, Henry was ripening eighty pallets of avocados per week (two thousand pounds per pallet), selling them as quickly as they became available. CAC soon began highlighting the pre-ripening process in its marketing.

Steve Barnard, founder and CEO of Mission Produce Inc., was the first to precondition fruit all the way to ripeness. "I went down to a local grocer here in South Oxnard, and I said, 'I'd like to do a trial with ripe avocados,'" explained Barnard. "The produce manager says, 'You're out of your mind.' I told him you have to be in this business. I said, 'Don't worry, whatever you sell is for you. If it's a mess, I'll personally clean it up. I'm going to bring you 10 boxes of ripe avocados on Friday and they're going to be ready to display with a sign that is higher priced than the unripe avocados, maybe 20 cents higher. I'll be back Monday. Just either clean it up or find out what happened.'"

Barnard returned to the store on Monday to find oranges where the avocados had been. "I was like, 'Where did all the avocados go?'" he remembered. "But the manager told me, 'Calm down. I sold out the ripe avocados by noon on Saturday.'" The hard avocados were still there. No one had bought any of those. I said to myself, 'Now we're onto something.'"

In 1993, Mission Produce built the first avocado ripening center, launching an "avocado ripe" program with Ralphs. Soon, Mission and other packinghouses were building or leasing ripening centers around the United States and Europe. Barnard calls pre-ripening one of three breakthroughs that led to the "avocado revolution" of the 2000s. (According to Barnard, the other two were the opening of the United States market under NAFTA and new avocado-related nutrition research.)

While pre-ripening is hardly perfect—fruit can deteriorate more quickly than naturally ripened fruit, especially if not done correctly—it was a game changer for avocado sales. Today, most avocados at U.S. supermarkets have gone through a pre-ripening process at the packinghouse, a distribution center or a local wholesaler.

Diana Kennedy on How to Choose an Avocado

Sometimes called the "Julia Child of Mexico," British food writer and cook Diana Kennedy introduced generations of Americans to authentic Mexican cooking in the 1970s and 1980s. Her recipes were based on her extensive travels around Mexico, where she lived for more than fifty years. Considered the world's foremost authority on Mexican cooking, her work was vital in preserving the country's authentic ingredients and techniques. In 2022, she passed away at age ninety-nine at her home in eastern Michoacán.

Diana Kennedy's 1989 book introduced millions of Americans to Mexican cuisine. *Author's collection.*

Among Kennedy's many publications, her *Art of Mexican Cooking* became the most famous book on the cuisine ever written when it first appeared in 1989. In it, Kennedy gives advice on how to select an avocado at the store. Her suggestions are as helpful as ever, especially her warning to avoid overripe avocados, a common mistake at the market or in the kitchen:

Avocados come into the markets in the United States underripe and should be bought ahead and ripened in a paper bag in a warm spot in the kitchen. An avocado at its best has flesh that feels firm and compact and just gives to the touch. If there is a hollow between the flesh and skin, try the next one. The final test: shake it. If the pit is loose, pass over that one. Even if it seems just right, you can cut one open and find the flesh mottled with brown patches; the flavor will have deteriorated. It is, therefore, always best to buy more than you need.

GROVE MANAGEMENT COMPANIES

There are few people better acquainted with the ins and outs of California's avocado industry than grove managers. Although growers founded the industry, many were not professional farmers. Instead, they depended on experts in avocado cultivation to care for their groves and manage the workers, mostly migrant laborers from Latin America. Grove management companies have been on the forefront of a host of issues, including testing new varietals or rootstocks, installing irrigation, disease and pest control, tree density experiments, soil and fertilizer studies and organic farming. They also have to be familiar with non-farming subjects, such as labor, immigration and regulatory compliance.

In the 1940s and 1950s, commercial growers began planting larger groves around the state. At the time, Calavo Growers was the dominant marketing organization. Along with its other services, it offered its members all-inclusive grove care. Calavo contracted with local management companies or relied on its own grove managers.

With the spread of independent handlers in the 1960s, grove care became something of a mandatory service offered to growers. Grove managers would contract directly with medium to large handlers. Some grove management companies became independent, accountable directly to growers rather than to handlers. They helped their clients with public agencies such as the Farm Bureau, UC Cooperative Extension farm advisors and county and state inspectors. Some of these companies even owned and managed their own groves in addition to those of clients.

Over the years, many of the most respected leaders within the industry have been grove managers. Prominent managers include Rick Shade, Carl Stucky and Scott Van Der Kar (Carpinteria); Doug O'Hara (Ventura); Sal Dominguez (Santa Paula); Charley Wolk, Mike Sanders, Jaime Serrato and Al and Jerome Stehly (San Diego County); Chuck Bandy and McMillan Farm Management (Temecula); and many more. They have served on association boards and received numerous awards for their service to the industry. They have lived through fires, droughts, root rot, price crashes, foreign imports, planting booms and busts, labor shortages, varietal controversies, water crises and more. Through it all, grove managers have remained the industry's strongest advocates, helping their clients grow the best avocados in the world.

....

Guacamole
From The Art of Mexican Cooking by Diana Kennedy, 1989

INGREDIENTS
3 tablespoons finely chopped white onion
1–2 serrano peppers, finely chopped*
2 rounded tablespoons finely chopped cilantro
Scant ½ teaspoon (or to taste) sea salt
3 large avocados (a little more than 1 ½ pounds)
⅔ cup finely chopped unpeeled grape tomatoes

THE TOPPING
2 tablespoons finely chopped white onion
1 heaped tablespoon finely chopped cilantro
2 tablespoons finely chopped grape tomatoes

Kennedy recommends using a molcajete (a traditional mortar and pestle) to grind the onion, peppers, cilantro and salt into a rough paste, but any bowl is fine. In the same bowl or molcajete, roughly mash the avocado, blending in the ingredients. Gently mix in the chopped tomatoes and sprinkle with onion, cilantro and more tomatoes if desired. Serve immediately.

*Kennedy's original recipe calls for four serrano peppers (with seeds!), which will make your guacamole impossibly spicy. Perhaps she was having fun at the expense of her American readers? Note the absence of citrus, which Kennedy insisted "spoils the balance of flavors." You may disagree.

THE AVOCADO REVOLUTION

2000-PRESENT DAY

Our industry has gone from this little oddity into a big, mainstream, global industry. It's just mind-boggling how fortunate we have been to find ourselves placed where we are.

—Rob Brokaw, 2024

The first decade of the new millennium marked the end of an era for the California avocado industry. After nearly one hundred years, Avocado Land had become Avocado World. Around the globe, countries were developing or expanding their own industries, usually with the help of California growers, packers, nurserymen and researchers. As of 2023, a dozen countries grow more avocados than California. Meanwhile, the slumbering giant of Mexico had finally awakened to become the world's dominant avocado player, with most of its fruit destined for America. Mexican exports to the United States rose from a few million pounds in 2000 to a few billion pounds in 2023.

The start of the millennium also witnessed the passing of two pioneers whose efforts had been critical to the industry. In 2004, Ralph Pinkerton, the first president of what became the California Avocado Commission—the industry's first association solely dedicated to marketing—died at age eighty-four. Thanks in part to Pinkerton's leadership and marketing genius, avocados went from being an exotic luxury fruit in a few dozen retail markets to a must-have staple in the produce section of nearly every grocery store in the nation. His marketing campaigns were the first to emphasize avocados'

Pictured together in the 1980s, Ralph Pinkerton (*left*) and Jack Shepherd (*right*) were indispensable pioneers of the avocado industry. *Courtesy of SBC/THL.*

nutritional benefits, epitomized by his groundbreaking ads in the late 1980s starring Angie Dickinson. He was also the first to use print and radio marketing tie-ins ads. As much as anyone, "Pink" helped catapult avocados into the public imagination.

Yet another blow to the industry occurred in 2006, when Calavo executive and longtime CAS yearbook editor Jack Shepherd passed away at age ninety-two. Since joining Calavo in 1933, Shepherd had risen through the ranks to become its president. During that time, he also served as editor in chief of the Society's yearbook, overseeing that highly influential journal for nearly fifty years. He received the Society's Award of Honor twice during his sixty-five-year career, putting him in the company of only five other pioneers. During his time, Shepherd acted as unofficial chief archivist, spokesperson and elder statesman. Through his passion, intelligence, hard work and affability, he did more than anyone to shape the industry into what it is today.

"Jack is our poet laureate," said Leonard Francis in a speech honoring Shepherd at the 1998 Society meeting. "He is not just a great writer and editor, he is our most eloquent writer and speaker. He has been a spotlight as well as a searchlight…he is our grand man."

In the two decades following 2000, the avocado industry would lose more grand men and women, including pioneering nurserymen Hank Brokaw and Oliver Atkins; handler Gil Henry; farm advisors Leonard Francis and Don Gustafson; scholars Charles Schroeder, George Zentmyer, Tom Embleton and Bob Bergh; and growers Sam Perricone, Ted and Lois Todd, Bill Arterberry and Bob Lamb, among many others. Each one prepared the way for the astounding and unexpected explosion of growth across all sectors of the avocado industry, not just in the United States but around the world.

Mexican Imports Send Demand Soaring

After NAFTA, there was an explosion in all things avocado, from cookbooks and health products to games, toys and clothing. To use today's lingo, avocados went viral. This may have been best epitomized by the sudden popularity of avocado toast in the 2000s, a phenomenon that swept across the world, fueled by the internet and social media. Celebrities, chefs and influencers posted photos and recipes online touting their version of a dish that had been around for nearly five hundred years.

Despite the dire predictions of hundreds of growers, leaders and lobbyists, Mexican imports did not decimate California's industry. On the contrary, the unimpeded flow of avocados from Mexico drove demand higher than anyone on either side of the border had anticipated, even as nominal avocado prices rose.

In 2001, California produced 400 million pounds of avocados, representing roughly 85 percent of all avocados consumed in America. Florida produced another 10 percent, with Chilean and Mexican imports making up the difference. That year, the average American's per capita consumption stood at roughly 2 pounds per year, more or less where it had been for the previous two decades. By 2011, Mexico was importing more than 60 percent of avocados and per capita consumption surged to 4 pounds. That same year, California produced a solid harvest of 450 million pounds, a number now representing only 30 percent of total consumption. In 2021, Mexico sent a whopping 2.4 billion pounds (triple the amount in 2011), approximately 92 percent of all avocados consumed. American per capita consumption ballooned to 8 pounds.

"In retrospect, I think imports have actually been a benefit to us," says Rick Shade, a longtime grower, grove manager and industry leader from Carpinteria. "I liken it to lettuce. Lettuce is in front of the consumer 365 days a year. When I was a kid, avocados were not. California was the only show in the country. When we had avocados, they were in front of the consumer. But when they were out of season, they weren't there. In the spring, we would essentially have to buy shelf space back in the grocery store. Now avocados are there 365 days, so it's on the consumer's mind all the time."

Today, while the rate of increase for both Mexican imports and American demand has slowed, it shows no signs of stopping. In 2022, America consumed 2.83 billion pounds of avocados, of which Mexican imports were responsible for 83 percent. With a lighter crop of 239 million that year, California avocados made up less than 8 percent of the total market. Peru was a distant third at 198 million pounds, with Chile, Colombia and the Dominican Republic all under 10 million. According to the Hass Avocado Board, imports have risen by 22 percent from 2022 to 2023. U.S. per capita consumption of avocados now exceeds 9 pounds.

One key concern among California growers in the wake of NAFTA was that an oversupply of avocados from Mexico would cause avocado prices to plummet. Since Mexico's input costs were and are vastly lower than those in California, many believed that the state's grower would not be able to compete. However, a collapse in avocado prices has not yet materialized. In fact, while the industry had long been subject to extreme price fluctuations, prices received by growers actually rose 22 percent from 2011 to 2018.

Whether real prices have kept pace with nominal prices is another matter. Hoy Carman's research on avocado prices between 1962 and 1994 indicates that while nominal prices rose significantly, real prices actually declined. Given the 82 percent cumulative inflation over the past twenty-four years, a similar decline in real prices has probably occurred since 2000.

AVOCADOS GO GLOBAL

The steady supply of high-quality fruit from Mexico has been a major part of the remarkable surge in demand for avocados. For millions of

Americans who lived west of the Rockies, finding avocados in local markets before NAFTA was difficult, if not impossible. Much of the state's fruit was consumed within California, which has always had a significant percentage of "super users"—that is, people who eat avocados at a far higher rate than the average person. Not surprisingly, when avocados began to arrive in large numbers in supermarkets in Pennsylvania, Michigan and New York, people purchased them more often. This growth in demand continued to rise as more sporadic users in the Plains states and the Northeast corridor gained greater access to year-round avocados.

Americans were not alone in their rising rates of consumption. Over the past twenty years, avocados have become an international phenomenon, with both supply and demand rising exponentially across the globe. By 2018, Latin America had more than 750,000 acres of avocados in production, mostly in Michoacán but also in Chile, Peru, Brazil, Colombia and the Mexican state of Jalisco. Production around the Mediterranean rose significantly as well, with 75,000 acres in Spain, Israel, Morocco and Portugal. Southern Africa, Kenya, Vietnam, Australia and New Zealand also increased production. A 2021 report by CIRAD estimates worldwide avocado plantings at 1,215,000 acres, 75 percent of which is in Latin America.

While the United States remains the world's biggest importer of avocados, even this might change by the end of the decade. Per capita consumption is now rising at a faster pace in the EU-UK market than in the United States, according to a 2021 study by the World Avocado Organization (WAO). Research shows that U.S. sales grew by 5.8 percent in 2020, while those in the EU-UK rose by 23 percent. Currently, North America accounts for approximately 1.2 million tons of annual imports, while EU-UK imports around 900,000 tons. So far, Asia has been the world laggard, with only 146,000 tons of avocados consumed in 2022. But even a small demand uptick in places like China, Japan, India and South Korea would be significant.

MORE REASONS FOR SKYROCKETING DEMAND

Immigration from Latin America

Another reason behind the spike in American demand for avocados was an explosion in immigration from Latin America—especially Mexico—over the past forty years. As one California grower put it, the Mexican population "has essentially blown out of the southwest and gone all over the country."

Mexicans are "super heavy" consumers of avocados, eating close to nineteen pounds per capita annually. Beginning in the 1950s, Mexican-born immigrants began entering the United States in large numbers, joining an already significant population of U.S.-born Hispanics. Between 1950 and 2000, the Latino population in the United States grew at a rate of 60 percent to 80 percent every decade. From 2000 to 2021, the Mexican-origin population increased by an average of 79 percent, from 20.9 million to 37.2 million. In the same period, Mexican foreign-born or immigrant population grew by 23 percent, from 9 million to nearly 11 million. As of 2021, there are approximately 60 million Hispanics, including 38 million of Mexican origin. Since avocados pervade Latin American cuisine—which in turn has become wildly popular in the United States—immigration has meant rising avocado consumption rates. Again, the trend shows no signs of slowing down.

Mexican Chain Restaurants

A related demand driver has been the proliferation of Mexican-themed chain restaurants. Franchises such as Chipotle, Taco Bell, Del Taco, El Pollo Loco and others represent some of the estimated 200,000 Mexican restaurants in the United States. Thanks to its famous guacamole, for example, Chipotle sold the equivalent of 130 million pounds of avocados in its 3,400 restaurants in 2024. Since 2020, Del Taco averaged over 2 million pounds of avocados in its 600 stores. El Pollo Loco sells more than 4.5 million pounds annually at its 500 locations. The popularity of avocado in sushi beginning in the 1990s (epitomized by the California and rainbow rolls) shows that Mexican food isn't the only cuisine utilizing the fruit.

Finally, "big box" wholesale warehouse stores such as Costco and Walmart helped drive demand. These large-volume stores made avocados widely available at below-average prices to millions of Americans. With six hundred stores in forty-eight states and Puerto Rico, Costco sells millions of pounds of avocados annually, sourcing organic and conventional fruit from Mexico, Peru, Chile, California and elsewhere. While Kroger and Aldi purchase more avocados than any other corporations in the world, other large grocery chains such as HEB, Albertson's and Publix purchase significant amounts as well. These days, it is not unusual to see three or four different displays of avocados at a typical grocery store.

Big box retailers like Walmart and Costco (pictured here) sell millions of pounds of avocados annually. *Photo by Rob Crisell.*

AVOCADOS ARE HEALTHY—AGAIN

Besides more supply, perhaps the most significant factor behind the increased avocado consumption among Americans has been the public's mounting awareness of the fruit's nutritional value.

Even before the founding of the industry in 1915, there were a handful of articles in non-scientific publications that praised the "nutritive" or dietetic aspects of the avocado. For the most part, however, propagators such as Rideout and Blake took charge of informing the public about the fruit's nutritional benefits, usually with no small amount of hyperbole.

At the initial meeting of the California Avocado Society in 1915, nutritionist and board member Myer Edward Jaffa presented a paper titled the "Food Value of the Avocado." Jaffa's article was based on his work at UC–Berkeley, where he served as head of the division of nutrition. Jaffa would act as the industry's unofficial nutritionist, publishing several pieces in the Society's yearbook and elsewhere. The modest goal of his inaugural article for the yearbook was to "offer some data" as to why the avocado "should not be considered merely as a relish." After analyzing the chemical makeup of a dozen different varieties, Jaffa compared his findings with other fruits based on each one's "nutritive value," including caloric value (especially fats), digestibility and dietetic value (minerals, vitamins and organic acids). He concluded that the avocado was "in a class by itself" because of its "far higher caloric value than any other fresh fruit," without the correspondingly high sugar levels.

By Calavo's founding in 1924, most in the media took for granted the goodness of avocados, even if the vast majority of Americans had never tried one. Nutrition-related articles in the yearbooks usually appeared under the heading of marketing and were rarely scientific or technical.

In her role as Calavo's assistant secretary and director of nutrition, Adeltha Peterson created many of the nutrition-related marketing materials in the 1930s and 1940s, like this from the 1930 yearbook:

M.E. Jaffa was the unofficial nutritionist for the California avocado industry through the 1930s. *Courtesy of SBC/THL.*

The Calavo is a food fruit.…Through their mineral and vitamin content, they are "protective," and regulate the body processes, figuring prominently in the coordination of the functions of nerves, glands, muscles, etc., enabling the body to use its available fuel and building material to the best advantage.…It is the only fruit which, unprocessed from the tree, gives man a flavorful food containing fruit-oil to energize his body.

Despite making sometimes inflated (or at least unproven) claims, Peterson and other industry leaders of the time anticipated many of the more sophisticated studies that would come along fifty years later. For example, Peterson notes that avocados are beneficial even for those on a "reduction diet," since high-oil avocados are extremely satiating and filled with "healthy fats." Peterson also crafted the Calavo marketing strategy that urged avocados as an ideal food for children: "The wise mother…is continually looking for a high source of energy for her children, as the growing boy of ten may require more energy food than his father."

Often, Peterson's claims about children's alleged fondness for avocados seem more like wishful thinking than reality. "See Johnny throw up his cap with enthusiasm or Junior College Audrey look with interest if you include a half of calavo with waxed paper," she wrote in a 1930s pamphlet titled *Calavos for the Home*. "If desired, you may include a little salt and a slice or two of lemon. However, in our tests with children in large groups, we find that these little connoisseurs like their calavos so well, they will eat them day in and day out, just as they come."

A Calavo ad from 1953 noted that avocados "are endlessly adaptable, blend[ing] with all fruits, vegetables, meats.…A wonderful food for babies and children." The ad encouraged the reader ("Mrs. Modern Housewife") to send off for free growth charts and recipes.

During the war years, Calavo tied the eating of avocados to the Allied effort in Europe. A 1942 spot stated that avocados are "rich in natural vitamins, minerals, and energy units so vital to Victory." The exchange sold millions of avocados to the U.S. Army and U.S. Navy during the war, giving out thirty-five thousand pamphlets on how to utilize them.

California Avocado Commission Fights the "Fat Police"

With the exception of these early marketing efforts, the industry largely ignored avocado nutrition after Professor Jaffa's passing in 1930. In fact, the

Society did not print another nutrition article for three more decades. At the time, few food writers or dietitians disputed the widely accepted idea that avocados were good for you.

In 1959–60, the price of avocados crashed. Most blamed the decline on a particularly heavy crop, as well as on a lack of sufficiently developed markets outside California. The price slump led to the formation of a new marketing association in 1960.

But another reason for the price slump may have been the negative publicity that avocados were suddenly receiving from the new "war on fat." As most contemporary nutritionists now acknowledge, the war on fat turned out to be a well-intentioned but mostly wrongheaded fiasco, likely contributing to today's high levels of obesity and diabetes. When it came to avocados, the war's defects were especially glaring.

Criticism of the avocado based on its high fat content—one of the fruit's main selling points for one hundred years—arose from new studies in the late 1940s that seemed to show a correlation between high-fat diets, high cholesterol levels and heart disease. These studies led many to conclude that a low-fat diet might prevent heart disease in high-risk patients. By the late 1950s, many nutritionists, food writers and government bureaucrats had decided that a low-fat diet was beneficial not just for high-risk heart patients, but for everyone. With twelve grams of fat and 125 calories per half-shell serving, avocados found themselves in the crosshairs of an American food fight.

In 1976, U.S. Congressional hearings resulted in a range of "solutions," including the first set of USDA dietary guidelines in 1980. These guidelines advised against consuming high-caloric foods, especially sources of saturated fats and cholesterol such as red meat, full-fat dairy, eggs and butter. Avocados were doubly suspect—they were not only high in calories for a fruit, but 75 percent of those calories also came from fat. Lost in the discussion was the fact that avocados contain mostly healthy monosaturated fats. Many even mistakenly believed that they contained cholesterol. For the first time, the American Heart Association put the avocado on its list of foods to avoid.

CAS members were quick to notice the change in public attitudes toward the avocado. In the 1959 yearbook, grower and physician Horace Pierce argued that sales were suffering because "the present-day housewife" thinks of an avocado as a "luxury item that is very fattening." Pierce lamented that "somehow the buying public has gained the idea that the avocado should be avoided because of this high caloric value and many women avoid them on this account alone."

Although not a nutritionist, Pierce adroitly outlined the vital differences between the mostly unsaturated, unhydrogenated fats in avocados and the saturated kind in animal products and processed foods. "It has been found that the oil of the avocado is one of the most valuable of the unsaturated fatty acids," he wrote. Far from raising cholesterol levels, avocados are among the most "desirable oils" since the oil contained in an avocado "is not a fattening agent so much as a protective anti-cholesterol factor that helps them to balance the really fattening and sometimes potentially harmful fats."

Following up on Pierce's article, the Society published a paper in 1960 by Wilson Grant, a biochemist at the University of Miami School of Medicine, on the "positive influence of avocados on serum cholesterol."

California Avocado Commission and Nutrition Research (1980–2007)

In 1962, CAC replaced Calavo as the industry's chief marketer. Under its first director, Ralph Pinkerton, the Commission took the lead in promoting the state's avocados. However, there was no money to pay for nutrition research. Most funds went to general marketing, varietal research, root rot and other issues of more pressing concern to the industry.

Fallbrook farm manager and grower Charley Wolk was instrumental in transforming avocado-related nutrition research within the industry. *Courtesy of SBC/THL.*

However, the war on fat had not gone away. In the 1970s, media "health experts" regularly accused avocados of containing not only unhealthy fats but also cholesterol. To combat such misinformation, CAC and Pinkerton devised what would become one of the most famous ad campaigns of the 1980s, using Angie Dickinson to promote the fruit as compatible with a beautiful figure. Although the well-known campaign did much to restore avocados' healthy reputation, negative perceptions and myths persisted.

Around the time of the Dickinson ad campaign, CAC formed the Nutrition Advisory Committee (NAC), enlisting the help of industry professionals as well as experts in the field of health and nutrition. Charley Wolk—a grower, agricultural manager and longtime industry leader from Fallbrook—served as the committee's chairman. From its founding until 2005, Wolk and the other committee members, including Dr.

David Heber, director of the UCLA Center for Human Nutrition, played a vital role in educating the public about the health benefits of avocados.

In 2005, Produce News honored Wolk for his work with the NAC, listing some of the committee's accomplishments, including an "exponential increase" in the number of positive health stories about avocados. "The percentage of Americans who consider avocados to be 'good for you' rose from 35 percent to 67 percent over roughly 20 years," stated the article. "And avocados have been featured as a 'Nutrition Superstar' in the American Diabetes Association's Food & Nutrition Bible." By 2007, when CAC handed off its leadership role in avocado nutrition to the Hass Avocado Board, the Commission's research had done much to re-convince the United States and the world of the fruit's essential goodness.

In the 2011 issue of CAC's quarterly publication *From the Grove*, longtime editor Tim Linden summarized the impact of Commission-funded research: "A true marker of the success of the CAC nutrition project is that with their status as a 'Super Food,' avocados are now featured in almost every popular diet....The fruit is listed as one of the most nutrient-dense foods, and its nutritional benefits are well accepted."

Hass Avocado Board and Nutrition Research since 2007

As discussed earlier, NAFTA's passage in 1997 marked the beginning of imported Mexican avocados to the United States. Within a decade, fruit from Mexico—as well as Peru, Chile, Dominican Republic and elsewhere— dwarfed that grown in California. Among other concerns, Californians thought it was unfair that foreign importers were profiting from nearly one hundred years of marketing and research efforts funded by the state's industry. Wolk and other leaders associated with CAC petitioned Congress to create another marketing association funded by fees generated from both domestic and foreign avocado sales.

As a result of these efforts, Congress passed the Hass Avocado Promotion, Research and Information Act (HAPRI) of 2000, which led to the creation of the Hass Avocado Board (HAB) in 2002. Under USDA supervision, HAB established an assessment rate of 2.5 cents per pound on all foreign and domestic avocado producers, with the goal of increasing American demand for Hass, regardless of its country of origin. Of these funds, marketing associations in member countries received 85 percent back, which they were required to use to market avocados in the United States. HAB fees generated

A recent in-store advertising display funded by "Avocados from Mexico." Since the creation of the Hass Avocado Board (HAB), avocado marketing in the United States has grown exponentially. *Photo by Rob Crisell.*

by California growers went to CAC, while fees generated by Mexican imports went to the Mexican Hass Avocado Importers Association.

With the remaining 15 percent of assessments, HAB's small staff in California coordinated marketing efforts to enhance those of CAC and other associations. In 2006 alone, the combined associations spent more than $35 million in marketing. In 2007, with the encouragement of CAC and the rest of the industry, HAB redefined its role to focus on two broad goals: developing more sophisticated U.S. market research and creating a nutrition program in support of avocado consumption.

In 2010, HAB created the Avocado Nutrition Center (ANC), funding research at various universities in avocado-related nutrition. Soon, there were new studies on the role of avocados in heart health, weight management and Type-2 diabetes treatment. Thanks to HAB and its senior director of nutrition Nikki Ford, American consumers became more aware than ever about how beneficial avocados really are.

"Before [2010], only nine publications existed in [avocado nutrition] literature compared to today, where there are more than 50 scientific publications," wrote Ford in the 2022 CAS yearbook. "Expanding our understanding of the avocado's health benefits is critical for providing consumers permission to indulge in avocado more often."

Growers and packers alike have heralded HAB as transformative for the industry. "The Hass Avocado Board is such an incredible vehicle," said Scott Bauwens, CEO of Simpatica, a commercial grower based in Santa Barbara. "It's the envy of the produce industry. The more avocados that come in, the more marketing dollars are funneled into the U.S. for nutrition research. We've got this pipeline of nutrition research that's elevating the demand and value of avocados. We also have this data system that's telling us how much is coming in, where it's coming in, so we can be more responsible with moving and receiving fruit."

CHALLENGES AHEAD

Expensive Water and Other Costs

While fruit prices have risen since 2000, California's avocado acreage has steadily declined, due to rising input costs associated with labor, land and taxes. However, it is the skyrocketing cost of water—long one of Southern California's most pressing issues—that has pushed many San Diego County avocado farmers to the brink.

Since 2010, the average price of water in the county has grown an astounding 8 percent annually. Part of the problem is that the San Diego County Water Authority (SDCWA) vastly overestimated future demand. For years, it built costly projects, from dams to new pipelines to a desalination plant on the coast. Yet by 2022, the region's water demand had dropped by 40 percent. Beginning in 2005, mandatory water conservation laws cut demand still further, spiking rates. Fewer farmers meant that fewer stakeholders shared the cost of water, which made already expensive water more so, leading to even fewer farmers. Small avocado growers and farmers of all types now find themselves caught in what some describe as a death spiral.

To make matters worse, the quality of the Colorado River water has become almost too salty for avocado trees, which are salt sensitive. Beginning around 2013, salt levels in the water rose by 20 percent, according to David Crowley, a soil scientist at University of California–Riverside. Treating water with reverse osmosis or blending is often too expensive for the average grower. Unless farmers have their own wells with good quality water, they must purchase already treated water at exorbitant prices from local water authorities.

As a result of these issues and others—particularly surging labor costs driven by high inflation and low unemployment—avocado acreage shifted from San Diego to the northern counties. As late as 2007, San Diego still had 26,000 acres of avocados. By 2022, that number had fallen to 12,367. Groves in the Temecula area have experienced a similar decline. Today, more than 66 percent of the state's avocados are located in the northern counties of Ventura, Santa Barbara and San Luis Obispo. While many large packinghouses remain in the south, the center of Avocado Land has moved north.

Thankfully, San Diego's water situation is set to improve in the near future. In response to their users' struggles, two northern water districts in the Rainbow and Fallbrook area chose to detach from SDWCA and join a water district in Riverside County. In 2023, after years of negotiation, the two local agencies agreed to pay SDWCA $25 million in exchange for detachment. Avocado farmers in Fallbrook and Rainbow—who own approximately 5,300 acres among them—should save more than 25 percent on water bills, even after settlement costs. With luck, the county's avocados may see a resurgence in the coming years.

The Mexican Dilemma

No one in the avocado industry denies the critical role that foreign avocados—more than 85 percent of which are from Mexico—has played in spiking American demand following NAFTA. The value of the annual avocado trade between the two countries now exceeds $3 billion, triple what it was in 2000. In 2021, the United States finally allowed growers in the Mexican state of Jalisco to start shipping fruit as well, ensuring even more avocados in the near future.

But an endless supply of avocados from Mexico has its downsides too. For years, many California growers have argued that Mexico's year-round fruit imports have kept avocado prices artificially low. In 2023, dozens of small- to medium-sized growers in San Diego County formed a group called the Avocado Growers of California to draw attention to the "unrestricted supply of foreign fruit," which they argue has "driven prices down to unsustainable levels." These growers reflect the fears of some that avocado cultivation in Southern California may be on the edge of extinction.

But Mexico has also come under fire for a host of ills unrelated to the quantity or quality of its fruit. In 2022, a week before the Super Bowl, the U.S. government abruptly banned all avocado imports from Mexico after a USDA inspector in Michoacán received a violent threat. The United States lifted the ban a week later when Mexican authorities promised to increase security at groves and packinghouses. The incident drew heightened attention to the warring drug cartels that have infiltrated and control much of Mexico's avocado industry. For years, criminal gangs in Michoacán and Jalisco have orchestrated kidnappings, extortion and murder to manipulate innocent farmers and take over avocado shipments. Americans are becoming increasingly aware that cartels are as invested in avocados as they are in illegal drug smuggling and human trafficking.

Since avocados are now an international industry, bad press about Mexico's avocados has the potential to negatively affect all avocados, including those grown in California.

A related issue generating bad publicity is the allegedly negative environmental impacts of avocado farming in various countries, including Kenya, Nigeria, Peru, Chile and elsewhere. However, it is Mexico's ongoing illegal deforestation of Michoacán and Jalisco that has drawn most of the world's attention. According to reporters at the *New York Times* and many other publications, a combination of cartels, landowners and corrupt public officials is illegally destroying pine oak and oyamel fir forests to make room for avocado cultivation. The international community has called on the Mexican government to halt the destruction of the country's precious resources. In the United States, environmental groups, California avocado growers and politicians hope to pass legislation that would require Mexico to adhere to the same climate, labor and sustainability standards that govern agriculture in the United States.

The issues facing Mexico's avocado industry seem daunting and may get worse before they get better. Recent American administrations have begun to explore imposing tariffs on steel and aluminum from Mexico. Perhaps avocados are next. Meanwhile, a small but growing number of avocado lovers around the world are expressing their fears that their favorite fruit is now morally problematic. A recent book gave a name to this newfound concern—"avocado anxiety."

Yet regardless of the problems in Mexico or in any other country, California avocados may be poised for of a new wave of growth and prosperity. In the final chapter, twenty-six of the leading citizens of Avocado Land share their ideas on how this wave may be taking shape.

....

Avocado Toast
Recipe by Rob Crisell, 2024

In the 2010s, Americans made avocado toast the most famous avocado-themed dish since guacamole. Millennials shared photos and recipes in millions of social media posts, turning the dish into one of the most searched items in social media history. Gwyneth Paltrow featured it prominently in her popular cookbook It's All Good *in 2015. For many, avocado toast symbolized a healthy diet and the California lifestyle. As the* Washington Post *put it, avocado toast is "more than just a meal—it's a meme."*

The recipe for avocado toast is simple—an open sandwich with smashed or sliced avocados on top, along with as many or as few other ingredients as desired. Australian chef Bill Granger may have been the first to include the dish on a restaurant menu in 1993. However, the origins of avocado toast go back to the first prehistoric Mesoamericans who piled avocado on a hot tortilla or—after the arrival of wheat flour with the Spanish—toasted bread.

One way that today's avocado toast differs from what the typical Aztec, Spaniard or early twentieth-century Californian enjoyed is the sheer number of additional ingredients besides avocado. These include feta, fried eggs, garlic salt, red chili flakes, radishes, tomatoes, scallions, sprouts, bacon, sunflower seeds, pomegranate seeds, sliced mango, dill, parsley, cilantro, jalapeños, citrus and more.

Here are my tips on making the perfect avocado toast. Don't worry—I won't take it personally if you stray from my recommendations to suit your own taste.

FIND THE BEST AVOCADOS. If you are near a farmers' market or a fruit stand in California, buy two locally grown, medium-sized avocados. Hass will do nicely, but if you find one of the lesser-known varieties, all the better. Make sure the fruit is ripe but not overripe, since this recipe calls for slices rather than mashed avocado.

PREPARE YOUR AVOCADO. On a cutting board, slice the avocado in half lengthwise, removing the pit. (Pro tip: always remove the cap or tiny remainder of the stem before cutting. Otherwise, it will end up in your dish.) With a Hass, you should be able to remove the peel from both halves with your fingers. Otherwise, scoop it out carefully with a large spoon. Place the half avocado face down at a slight angle. Use a sharp knife to thinly slice it widthwise, keeping the slices together. Gently push the slices down to create a straight row, like spreading out a deck of cards.

TOAST AND OIL YOUR BREAD. I prefer sourdough, but a hearty bread of any kind works well. Make sure the piece will accommodate your avocado slices. Once you toast the bread, brush the side on which the avocado will sit generously with olive oil or avocado oil.

PLACE THE AVOCADO ON YOUR TOAST. With a spatula or knife, put your avocado slices on the toast. Push them down gently so that the avocado adheres to the bread. Sprinkle a little more oil on the avocado and a pinch of coarse kosher salt. I like to add a few pinches of red chili flakes and a few drops of fresh lime juice or hot sauce. If you're in the mood for protein, top your toast with a fried egg or two.

THE FUTURE OF CALIFORNIA AVOCADOS

Avocados are a typical California story. Whether it be Silicon Valley or the movie industry or whatever, good things come out of California, and one of the best fruits or vegetables in the last 100 years has been avocados.

—Bob Lucy

More than a century after its founding, the California avocado industry finds itself at a crossroads. The citizens of the Golden State did more than anyone to introduce the United States and then the world to this delicious, nutritious green fruit. What growers, handlers and scholars lacked in numbers, they made up for in hard work, expertise and enthusiasm. Today, dozens of countries around the world boast their own industries, as the demand for avocados continues to skyrocket. Meanwhile, the avocado's role as California's state fruit is secure. Over the past year, I have had the honor of interviewing many of those who have dedicated their lives to California avocados. In this final chapter, they share their hopes, concerns, ideas and other observations about the future of Avocado Land.

Greg Alder (grower, writer)
Mary Lu Arpaia (UC–Riverside)
Steve Barnard (CEO, Mission Produce)
Scott Bauwens (CEO, Simpatica)
Gary Bender (former farm advisor)
Rob Brokaw (CEO, Brokaw Nursery)
Lee Cole (CEO, Calavo Growers)
Jan DeLyser (former executive, California Avocado Commission)

Sal Dominguez (grower, grove management)
Emiliano Escobedo (director, Hass Avocado Board)
Ben Faber (farm advisor)
Eric Focht (UC–Riverside)
Ralph Foster (grower)
Julie Frink (horticulturist)
Robert Jackson (grower)
Bob Lucy (former president, Del Rey Avocado)
Gray Martin (horticulturist)
Mike Sanders (S&S grove management)
Jaime Serrato (Serrato Farms)
Rick Shade (Shade farm management)
Al Stehly (Stehly grove management)
Jerome Stehly (Stehly Farms Organics)
Steve Taft (CEO, Eco Farms)
Scott Van Der Kar (grower, grove management)
Rob Wedin (former executive, Calavo Growers)
Charlie Wolk (Bejoca grove management)

SAN DIEGO COUNTY

When people drive around, they see the abandoned avocado groves. The trees are dead, all the leaves are gone, the weeds are growing, and so forth. It's like getting slapped in the face. But they'll drive right past five acres that's got small trees on it and never even notice it. There are investors coming in that aren't influenced by the emotional cost of water. They do their due diligence and they say that's not bad at all. I don't think acreage in San Diego County will continue to decline. It will, for want of a better word, stabilize or flatten.

—*Charley Wolk*

I think here in San Diego it's always going to be tough. There's not a lot of big groves around, and they're going to get developed. They're going to go out of business. I mean, there are groves that have wells, there's property, there's still land. I mean, it's a passion to stay in this business. But it's really going to be hard to keep the avocado business going in San Diego County.

—*Mike Sanders*

Lee Cole is among the largest individual avocado growers in California and is the longtime CEO of Calavo Growers. *Courtesy of Calavo Growers.*

The reason the groves shifted from San Diego County to the north is water. It was all about water. In San Diego, it's not the avocado problem. It is not because they're not selling. It's not because they're not a good price. It's because they can't grow them there because it's too expensive. Well, we don't have to do anything to water here [in Ventura County]. There's enough room in this valley to double our avocado production. The lemons will finally leave and they'll be replaced just like everything else. If the price stays similar to what it is, I think you're going to see California not too far out from 500 million pounds. I think you're going to see a big increase in growing. It's happening right now.

—*Lee Cole*

CALIFORNIA QUALITY

Well, the highest consumption in the United States is right here in California. It only has to go a hundred miles from where it's picked. It's going be in a better condition than something that has to travel 3,000 miles. My mother lives in Phoenix, and she said three out of five of the avocados she buys are blackened from handling mismanagement and travel. That has got to turn off growers and consumers. So the market is here in California, the fruit is here in California.

—*Ben Faber*

Believe me, the consumers now are getting more and more educated. A few years back, an avocado was an avocado. They all look alike. You know a lot of these retailers will stay on California as long as they can because of the quality. If you eat a Peruvian avocado and you really are an avocado eater and if you love avocados, you won't want it. You want California or Mexican. I think consumption for sure can double. I'm talking about worldwide now, but definitely it could double. It'll double in California. It'll double in the United States, too. It'll double every place.

—*Lee Cole*

California in general is growing a quality avocado, kind of like a fine wine. You can get the public to pay more, but it gets to a point where a certain number of people are going to say, "Well, I don't know. That's 65 cents for an avocado versus a buck and a half."

—*Ralph Foster*

I'm bullish about the industry. I think that California has developed a nice niche. We are local, and any local produce is always going to get a better demand in season than anywhere else. We have better quality, better shelf life. We're always going to get a premium. What speaks better to California than California avocados?

—*Scott Bauwens*

WATER

In San Diego County, water was always a key issue. It has just intensified over the years. Water is about 90 percent of the cost of production of avocados. The amount you spend on labor and fertilizer, even property taxes, is small compared to the cost of the water today. In 1972, water was about $75 per acre foot in Northern San Diego County. Now that same water is over $2,000 an acre foot. You look at these bigger groves—20 acres, 40 acres—their monthly water bill is five digits!

—*Charley Wolk*

My favorite issue—getting people to change irrigation management. They're on these schedules. They irrigate every Friday and run it for 30 minutes, because if it runs for 40 minutes, they're going to get a huge water bill. I keep preaching here—you're not saving money, you're saving your trees. Irrigate with the adequate amount of water for that area that you've got acres and you don't have enough water for eight. Cut out those two acres. People have been scrimping, especially down in San Diego, where water prices are so high. I keep harping on trees being an investment. You've got to spend money to make money. If you can't put enough water on to satisfy those trees' needs, get out of it.

—*Ben Faber*

I think the biggest problem is the water. Everybody knows that if we were paying $600 an acre foot, most of those growers would still be in business. And nobody is protecting our water for farmers. That's frustrating for me. I don't follow politics. I don't like politics. I don't believe in politics. I like to do things and politicians don't do things. There's not another California that you can say, "We're going to move all this to Colorado, to New York because there's lots of water there." The climate's here, everything that we need is here. They should be protecting the water, and nobody's doing anything on that. It's not like we farmers are building houses. We're providing food.

—Jaime Serrato

The really good thing about having avocado groves is that they make great neighbors. Minimal spraying—maybe once a year or not at all. Minimal cultivation, so you don't have a lot of dust. You don't have a lot of noise. You typically have harvest once per year. Another real plus is replenishment of groundwater. Because you just don't see rainwater running off much. I think with that leaf mulch, you've got this big sponge that just soaks it up. Compare that to something like strawberry fields that are going to be covered with plastic so that water is going to run off. Yes, avocados need a lot of water, but groves do more to replenish the ground water than other crops, and certainly more than hardscape.

Another reason that avocados make good neighbors is that groves are good fire buffers. That is a big deal now with wildfire resiliency. There's a group in Santa Barbara that is coming together and getting other groups to recognize those things that slowed down or stopped the Thomas fire and other fires from getting into the community. And one of those things is irrigated agriculture, which around here means avocado groves. When the fire is coming out of the dry brush, an avocado grove just slows it down or stops it.

—Scott Van Der Kar

Labor and Immigration

I'm a grower and a farm manager in the Valley Center area. All kinds of labor is needed and all of it comes from Mexico. There's not enough labor up here now to pick all the crops. My permanent workers live here year-round. We do supply housing and stuff like that for them. These people are smart. They know what they want. They want a good lifestyle. They want to be happy. What's life about? It's not about money. It's about being happy and about living. I take that from the Mexican culture.

In the beginning, my brothers and I worked alongside the laborers. Every summer we'd plant 40 or 50 acres of avocados and we had to dig the holes and dig the ditches with the guys. I don't know who was complaining—one of my brothers or maybe it was me—and somebody said, "Why do we have to do this?" And my dad said, "Because if you don't know how fast you need to go or how hard the work is, you can't tell the guys how fast to go when you're in charge. You get in that ditch."

—*Jerome Stehly*

With Mexican Americans, there's a certain understanding and connection with the earth. It's kind of second nature for most of the people in Mexico growing up. I think the connection to the earth is a lot stronger. I've always had passion for what I do. I like that we're providing food for people.

—*Jaime Serrato*

THE IMPACT OF MEXICO

We used to look at the growers in Fallbrook, Temecula, and Escondido as competition. However, with the onset of imports—beginning with Chile and then Mexico—we really kind of unified and it became us versus them. I remember going to meetings, you know, big rallies and protests against the importation of Mexican fruit. But the camel's nose was in the tent when the Chileans started showing up. In retrospect, though, I think that the imports have actually been a benefit to us.

—*Rick Shade*

We have increased consumer consumption, and that's certainly a good thing. Part of the cost is that they're putting the California growers out of business. I mean, they're correct that they have done a good job of promoting Mexican Hass. And even the fruit from Chile in the winter really has put avocados in front of consumers all year long. But you know the growers just have to either deal with these high water prices or they've got to have higher prices for their fruit. And Mexico is not allowing that.

—*Gary Bender*

Gary Bender is a retired farm advisor and avocado researcher from Fallbrook. He is the editor of the influential *Avocado Production in California* handbook. *Photo by Rob Crisell.*

It's no secret that a large segment of the Mexican avocado industry is run by cartels. This is the cartel's opportunity to reinvest their drug money in a way that essentially sanitizes their drug profits. Cleansing drug profits is not my idea of sustainability. So, we're at a real crossroads. If we don't do something fairly dramatic and soon, the small to medium avocado grower in California will be out of business in four years.

—Robert Jackson

Marketing and Sales

I think the marketing of CAC has always focused on the attributes that differentiate California avocados from the Mexican avocados, and others. What we really tried to do was to tell the story of why it is important to buy locally grown avocados. We always promoted California avocados. It didn't matter whether it was a GEM or a Pinkerton or whatever. I can say during my time at the Commission we were able to generate a profit and we were able to do the right things from a marketing standpoint. But it's never enough, at least from a grower standpoint. You have got to have respect for the growers—it's their money—and I always felt like it was never enough.

—Jan DeLyser

The success of the Hass Avocado Board in cultivating demand for Hass avocados has grown steadily over the past two decades. Through innovation, dedication, and a commitment to excellence, we have ripened the market for success and transformed it. I think it demonstrates that with vision and persistence, even the smallest seed can flourish into a global sensation.

—Emiliano Escobedo

For 50 years, all my brain ever thought about was avocados. I was interested in what I call the meat and potatoes of the business, which had to do with sales operations. How does this thing really work? It really had nothing to do with marketing. I don't really believe in marketing. I believe in avocados. You've got to buy them and you've got to sell them. It's a business.

Rob Wedin is a retired Calavo sales executive and industry leader with fifty years of avocado experience. *Courtesy of Calavo Growers.*

But it's not like selling pillows. You've got to get that stuff under your fingernails. You're managing perishable commodities every day. What are you going to quote the grower? What are you going to charge the customer? Are you going to make money? How much from Mexico are you going to bring in? Where are you going to bring it into?

—*Rob Wedin*

I think Del Rey has done a good job of trying to find the best customers in the country that will pay more money per box for California avocados. That's our job—to get more money for California growers. What we've done by going organic, finding these customers across the country that really care about quality and will pay for it.

—*Bob Lucy*

We could sell the entire California crop in state. As a grower, I don't care whether you sell it in California or Des Moines, Iowa. You give me the money, that's fine by me. Forget about everybody else. That's slowly but surely happening.

—*Charley Wolk*

I'm bullish about the industry. I think that California has developed a nice niche. We are local, and any local produce is always going to get a better demand in season than anywhere else. We have to be smart where we market. We're not going to market all the way to the East Coast. The majority of our fruit will be marketed right here in California.

—*Scott Bauwens*

NUTRITION

When we got the Hass Avocado Board started, the stuff they've been able to do as far as nutritional things—I mean, the demand just soared. When all the bad press would come out, CAC would attack it, but they would do it from a promotional-advertisements perspective. They didn't really do any real studies. They couldn't afford to do the studies. When HAB came along, there was so much money available that they were able to start hiring universities and nutritionists. They were really pushing the nutritional thing, and they got the American Heart Association finally to come through. It was just amazing the results that were coming out of the universities. We would always be bringing nutritionists out to the ranches.

—*Mike Sanders*

Avocado Varieties

Julie Frink has been a volunteer horticulturist and "avocado queen" since 1992. *Photo by Rob Crisell.*

At one time, we had 200 different varietals at the South Coast Research and Extension Center, and so many of them I grafted. I found them in somebody's yard and brought them in. If I have a specialty, it's the varieties. I found out I was more interested in historic varieties than in testing stuff from the breeding fields. If 400 people in California have Sharwils, that's just great. I wouldn't want all of a sudden for there not to be a Fuerte just because they're not commercial. They're so darn good! I just like varieties and I want them out there. It would be a shame for a good variety to be lost forever, and I'm sure a lot of them have been. In May, my favorite varietal is Jan Boyce. In July, it's Hellen, in the fall it's probably Fuerte and Reed, and in the spring, I like Pinkerton.

—*Julie Frink*

Hass—that's what the customer wants. When you've got a Cadillac, if you will, there's no pressure to change. You've got a perfect fruit, so to speak. You can pick Hass in this valley 12 months out of the year.

—*Lee Cole*

I think GEM is a good avocado and it produces heavy. Anything you can plant high density is a plus. The GEM is great because it produces young and it's an upright tree. I'm a huge believer.

—*Jaime Serrato*

The GEM is a good piece of fruit. The only problem is that there have been other varieties over the years. It's been hard to convince a retailer to try to teach the consumer about a new varietal. The biggest buyers of off-brand fruit have always been farmer's markets or small stores.

—*Jerome Stehly*

My dad was one of the first avocado growers in the state of California to plant Reed avocados. He was a neurosurgeon in the Navy and following his retirement from the Navy, he went into private practice in Fallbrook. He started growing avocados back in the mid- to late

1960s. Today, I have six avocado ranches and two citrus ranches that are located in Pauma Valley, Valley Center, Escondido, and Fallbrook. For me, planting Reeds is a family tradition, and I love the taste of a good Reed. It's just a phenomenal piece of fruit. There's just nothing like them.

—Robert Jackson

My cousin up in Washington is a foodie who loves avocados. When I visited him a couple years ago he had some avocados on his counter. A few were Hass, but one was a Fuerte. I was shocked, but it was unmistakably a Fuerte. I looked at the stickers on the fruit—all said they were from Mexico and all had a Hass PLU code. It was a Fuerte that had apparently stowed away in a shipment of Hass. I asked my cousin if he knew the Fuerte was a Fuerte. He had no idea. I cut it open and showed him the slightly larger seed with a pointier tip. We ate it together and it was good. Any talk about consumers wanting Hass and Hass only is hogwash. Avocado eaters want quality. Give them quality of any good variety, and do so year-round, and you're in business for a long time.

—Greg Alder

AVOCADO BREEDING

When Bob Bergh retired, they were going to shut down the breeding program, but I really believed that we need new varieties. I mean, we always have to be moving forward. I went to my department chair and said, "You really can't close down the program," and I listed all these reasons. By the time I took over the program [in 1997], they had identified about eight or nine different interesting things that could be released. The Luna is the last one of all these. Luna has a different texture than Hass in my book. It's smoother. In my mind, when I take stuff from the breeding home, it has to be able to make a good bowl of guacamole. I can tell you that Luna makes a dynamite bowl of guacamole.

—Mary Lu Arpaia

The question is, how are you going to improve Hass? Is one variety going to fit into all of these different systems? Probably not. It'll fit into a couple of them and not another one. This is what I talk about when I talk about germplasms and holding onto your diversity. It's like you're on a stepping stone going down a path. The wider that stepping stone is, the more directions you have if you step off of it.

From the perspective of our germplasm, we want to keep that step as wide as possible because you can't tell exactly what the future might hold. Pathogens mutate very quickly compared to trees, especially a monocultural clonal tree.

—*Eric Focht*

Hass is so dominant that there's some confusion, because if you're breeding, what are you looking for? You're looking for something that's more Hass than Hass is. And how do you achieve that? We're a little bit hamstrung because we don't even know what better-than-Hass looks like. Is it where the skin just falls off of the fruit? Or the seed is really small? Maybe it would be something that has a longer storage capability or a slightly better distribution of sizes?

—*Rob Brokaw*

Organic Farming

Doing organic—that's a bitch. Because you can only use certain things. You can't use any synthetic pesticides or herbicides. It makes it really hard. Sometimes the weeds will be half as high as the trees, but we won't cut them until we felt like it's kind of the last hoorah for the weeds. The labor costs just eat you alive.

—*Ralph Foster*

We still believe in organic. When we started, we didn't know we were going to get a premium. A lot of the new guys do it because they make more money. We think it's better for the soil, better for the planet, better for people. For avocados, there's probably less differentiation between conventional and organic. Even conventional farmers use very few chemicals compared to some other crops. If you do it right, organic growing can be every bit as good as conventional. We have groves that produce really well that are organic. When we first started, we were growing it organic and it was just us saying it was organic. People had to trust you. Today, it's way more regulated.

—*Steve Taft*

Learning from Other Countries

When I first went to Chile, I saw new ideas. High-density growing was one of them, but also much tighter management, higher manipulation of trees, higher intervention in terms of pruning and girdling. Some of these concepts originated in Israel. Reuben Hofshi was really the one that started preaching the gospel of high density here. But they were first implemented on a large scale in Chile. That opened my mind a little bit and enabled me to not be so partisan in my view of California in contrast to the rest of the world.

—*Rob Brokaw*

If you look at California's avocado growing versus the world, countries like Mexico, Peru, Chile, Israel, South Africa, New Zealand and all these areas in comparison are more advanced at maximizing yield. There are innovations happening in the world—understanding water and when the tree is at stress; understanding what's efficient water use and what's not; what is overwatering and what is under watering; understanding soils, inputs, and topsoil replenishment. There's still not a very good sense of that here in California, because we have a fractured industry, meaning the average grove size is six and a half acres. Growers need to focus on the business of growing avocados. They need to constantly improve and innovate. Those are the growers that are staying ahead in any business. You have to evolve.

—*Scott Bauwens*

FARMING

I do farm calls. I backstop the professionals that are out there in the field. I'm able to bring in information to help them do their jobs better. I deal directly with growers, and I deal more commonly with pest control advisors. I do research. But I'm more of a librarian. I call myself an agricultural psychologist—I listen to the issues and try to help people find their own solutions. Everyone's in a different situation. That's my main responsibility—communicating how to better manage a crop.

—*Ben Faber*

You have to have a lot of patience with an avocado. I think the biggest problem people make with avocados is picking them too early in the season. One story you always hear is people who say, "Oh, I've grown that variety of avocado and it was just horrible." Well, that's because you picked it six months too early. But if you're growing for commercial, you want get it off the tree as soon as the packers are ready. That's why many avocados in the market are bad. They are sometimes in cold storage for days and days. But if you pick an avocado off your tree and you let it soften, it's going to be a lot better.

—Julie Frink

Well, there are a lot of challenges, but growers aren't facing up to them. I think the Avocado Growers of California is an attempt to educate people or invite people to start solving common problems. But it's often alien for growers to express their own personal opinions. Growers are typically independent; they quietly attend meetings to learn from speakers. I think that the instructional system changed from the old University of California Cooperative Extension–style of reporting field observations to one that is research and data-driven. Research is typically narrowly defined, lengthy, and data can be misinterpreted. In reality, most farm problems are solved on the farm and they're solved by farmers, ingenuity, and experience. I think the industry should be grower-directed, not research-directed.

—Gray Martin

HIGH DENSITY AND OTHER INNOVATIONS

I started high density cold turkey back in 1972. There was no research or anything. I just looked at these small groves and said, wait a minute. If I plant these trees 15 by 20—which was the standard thing—I don't get very many trees. I decided I would plant new groves 12 by 12. That high-density set up has now been verified by research and experience, but I did it just because it seemed to make sense.

—Charley Wolk

Rob Brokaw shared with me the amazing attributes of the GEM avocado tree. That is the tree I am now planting in all my ranches. It offers the California grower a unique opportunity to produce an amazing piece of fruit at a high yield per acre in a high-density format. Industry average for Hass trees is about 6,000 pounds per acre. With my high density GEM planting, I am getting an average 25,000 pounds per acre.

—Sal Dominguez

Pickers get paid by the piece. So the more they can harvest, the more they get paid, and it's so much easier for them to do these high density groves. I mean, I proved that you can get higher yields with high density groves. I proved that we can pay the water bills in Valley Center with this. But then growers say, well, you've got more labor going on now, and the labor's getting expensive. They're right about that.

—*Gary Bender*

At Rancho Guejito, there are about 250 acres of avocados. We do high density, approximately 430 trees per acre. High density is the way to go. It just seems more efficient. That's one of the reasons we went to the high density, to make it easier to harvest. But it is more labor intensive. We've got so many trees that we're pruning year-round just to keep up. We're committed to making it work. We're teaching ourselves how to make it work.

—*Al Stehly*

One of the things we tried to control here was the cost of water and pumping it up to the groves on this mountain. I saw a long time ago that power was going to be something that we couldn't control, even if we got well water. So, I started doing solar 20 years ago on a lot of farms and it's paid off very well.

—*Jerome Stehly*

GEMs and Reeds are really the two varieties of avocados that are most conducive to high density planting because of the structure of the tree. We want to keep the trees in the eight to 10-foot range in height, primarily because of the canopy. It's critically important that you get sunlight into all areas of the trees in order to get production.

—*Robert Jackson*

AVOCADOS AT THE CROSSROADS

The future of California avocados is bright, but it won't be an easy road. There are the challenges coming from every direction—scarcity of skilled labor, the cost and availability of water, all the regulations we deal with every day, competition from foreign imports that seem to overwhelm us. California producers need to adapt to the challenges and find innovative ways to be more efficient, productive, and sustainable. A very wise agronomist out of South Africa once told me that there is not enough plantable ground for avocados in the world to meet the demand that is coming in the near future. I am very bullish on the future of our industry.

—*Sal Dominguez*

I think we're going to see avocado growing shift, just like it did with citrus. When I got hired [in 1983], citrus was 40 percent of the industries within the San Joaquin Valley and 60 percent of the industry was in Southern California. Now about 80 percent of the industry is in the San Joaquin Valley and 20 percent is in Southern California. The acreage didn't change that much, but it is redistributed. And I think that's probably what we'll see with avocados over time. I think the acreage will stay about the same, but it's going to redistribute.

—*Mary Lu Arpaia*

With this new crop coming, we're going to have three years in a row with harvests between 200 and 270 million pounds. That's really low by historical levels. It's half of what we used to produce. I hope that we can keep it at 200 million plus because if it gets too much below that, California becomes sort of a non-factor. Even at 200 million, you're not really a huge player. I just worry about the size of the industry and all those factors.

—*Steve Taft*

When I look at the California avocado industry, I think we do need to stay prepared for potential challenges with rising costs and from regulations. However, I see a greater opportunity as consumption continues to grow globally. California has a window in the market, since the harvest is mostly offseason from the Mexico season. Avocados are a known superfood, and with the fruit being versatile, it can be consumed at any meal. The key for success as a California grower is to maximize production.

—*Steve Barnard*

Bob Lucy (*left*), Jan DeLyser (*center*) and Steve Barnard (*right*) attend a recent Hass Avocado Board event. Lucy is the former president and founder of Del Rey Avocado. DeLyser was CAC marketing director for two decades. Barnard is the founder and CEO of Mission Produce, the largest avocado producer in the world. *Courtesy of HAB.*

I don't think the industry is at an apex, but it does seem to be at a crossroads. Right now, I don't see revolutionary technologies or market growth that will drive an accelerated boom. There are some advances in different corners of the industry. Some efforts are going to fail, some efforts are going to succeed. I think that our fortunes hinge on our ability to recognize those things that work and our willingness to implement them.

—*Rob Brokaw*

....

California Caprese Salad
By Rob Crisell

This is my Golden State twist on the classic dish. The trick here is to slice the avocados width-wise to create round pieces, but crescent-shaped slices work too.

INGREDIENTS
2 medium ripe avocados, sliced per directions
2 medium ripe tomatoes, sliced ¼-inch thick
Course sea salt
½ cup packed fresh basil leaves
8 ounces fresh mozzarella cheese, cherry size (Ciliegine)
Freshly ground black pepper
Red chili flakes
2 tablespoons extra-virgin olive oil
Optional: Red wine vinegar

Cut avocados width-wise and carefully remove pit and peel. Slice avocados widthwise to create circular or donut-shaped pieces. Arrange tomato slices on plate. Season with salt. On top of each tomato, place a basil leaf and an avocado slice. Place a cherry-size mozzarella ball inside the hole or depression of the avocado. Season with salt, black pepper, and chili flakes. Drizzle with olive oil and a splash of red wine vinegar, if desired. Serve immediately.

HOW TO GROW AN AVOCADO TREE

With Rob Brokaw (Brokaw Nursery)

Rob Brokaw is the owner of Brokaw Nursery, the largest commercial producer of avocado trees in the United States. For decades, his father, Hank, was a pioneering leader in the avocado industry, developing clonal root rot–resistant trees. Today, Brokaw Nursery and its avocado groves at Long Canyon Ranch in Santa Paula are at the heart of innovations related to high-density planting, water conservation, pruning techniques and sustainability. The following are Rob's expert tips on how to plant an avocado tree:

Proper field planting and early management of avocado trees are important in getting an orchard off to a running start. There are a few general principles to keep in mind:

- To avoid drying out, plant your trees as soon as possible after leaving the nursery.
- Planting on mounds or berms will yield great benefits and make trees easier to care for.
- Design irrigation systems so that relatively brief (4 to 6 hours) irrigation cycles can be applied two or three times per week.
- Mulching will be a big help in managing soil moisture and temperatures.
- Try to maintain a constant awareness of the trees' circumstances: atmospheric temperatures and humidity; soil moisture, texture and drainage characteristics, etc.
- The best growers can look at a tree and know whether it is "happy" or not.

Rob Brokaw (*left*) and longtime CAS board member Carl Stucky at Brokaw's ranch in Santa Paula. Stucky presented Brokaw with the Society's 2023 Award of Honor. *Courtesy of Wayne Brydon.*

PLANTING is an important operation and if done properly the trees will develop rapidly. The hole should only be about 12" in diameter and no deeper than the height of the soil surface in the nursery pot. The field soil should not be excessively wet or dry. It's best to work with only the native soil, not with added mulches. The tree is lowered into the hole so that the top surface of the nursery soil is about 1" above the field soil level (it will settle a little bit in the first few weeks), the plastic pot removed, and native soil filled in around the tree. Take care to tamp the soil thoroughly and to ensure that there are no air pockets in the soil profile (these will inhibit root growth). Finally, a very thorough drenching irrigation will settle the soil and give the tree a great start.

IRRIGATION is the easiest aspect of tree management to get wrong. Understanding that the tree's functional roots are mostly located in the upper foot of the soil profile makes it easy for us to focus our efforts on maintaining correct moisture levels in that critical band. Soil that remains too wet or too dry for too long will cause root damage, so we look to apply relatively frequent irrigations that don't reach to the soil's lower depths but still provide adequate moisture to the stratum where the roots reside. The objective is to maintain soil moisture at a level that ensures water is available to the roots but not saturated—oxygen needs to be present and available in the tiny air pockets in the soil. Every two months or so, depending on water quality, apply an extra-long irrigation cycle so that salts leach away from the roots. Drippers and mini-sprinklers are both commonly and successfully used.

NUTRITION is difficult to implement with precision. Analyze leaf and soil samples once per year and make a nutrition plan derived from that information with assistance from a laboratory, if possible. The principal objectives are to mitigate chemical imbalances and to ensure the presence of enough critical fertilizer elements. There are a number of other decisions that a grower must make, such as planting distances and strategies for pruning and girdling trees for productivity. There are many correct approaches. In general, growers who keep their trees healthy and happy—and who recognize when their trees are in distress—tend to be the most successful.

PLACES, PRODUCTS AND EVENTS

Here are some shops, websites and festivals that feature California avocados.

FESTIVALS

FALLBROOK AVOCADO FESTIVAL. The world's longest-running avocado festival takes place every April in downtown Fallbrook. www.fallbrookchamberofcommerce.org; (760) 728-5845.

CALIFORNIA AVOCADO FESTIVAL. One of the largest festivals in Santa Barbara County, the California Avocado Festival takes place in Carpinteria every October. www.avofest.org; (805) 684-0038.

A poster from the 2017 California Avocado Festival in Carpinteria. *Courtesy of California Avocado Festival.*

ASSOCIATIONS AND WEBSITES

THE CALIFORNIA AVOCADO COMMISSION. CAC is the main marketing association for California growers. Its site has information on all things related to the avocado, including grower profiles and tips on ripening, recipes, growing, nutrition and more. www.californiaavocadogrowers.com.

THE CALIFORNIA AVOCADO SOCIETY. The oldest avocado organization in the world, the Society represents avocado growers in California and elsewhere. Its annual yearbooks chronicle the century-long history of the industry. www.californiaavocadosociety.org.

THE HASS AVOCADO BOARD. As a research and promotion board for Hass avocados in the United States, HAB focuses on funding and conducting nutrition research, as well as creating production and consumption data. www.hassavocadoboard.com.

AVOCADOSOURCE. This site is an excellent resource for everything related to avocados. Created by the Hofshi Foundation, the site serves as an archive for most of the Avocado Society's annual yearbooks. www.avocadosource.com.

UC–RIVERSIDE AVOCADO VARIETY COLLECTION. A good resource for those who want more technical information about avocados. www.avocado.ucr.edu.

THE YARD POSTS. Greg Alder is a Master Gardener located in Ramona, California. His site includes advice on growing different plants and trees, especially avocados. Greg's detailed profiles of the many avocado varieties are especially worthwhile. www.gregalder.com.

FACEBOOK has a number of pages related to California avocados, including "Southern California Backyard Avocado Growers," "California Avocado and More" and "California Avocado Growers."

SHOPS AND DESTINATIONS

RANCHO VASQUEZ. This historic, family-owned avocado farm in Azusa is open to the public in the spring and summer. www.ranchovasquez.com.

AVOCADO TEA COMPANY. Sharon Colona and her husband, Scott Wibbenmeyer, make natural tea from California avocado leaves, sourced from their grove in Temecula and elsewhere. Products are available in stores or online. www.avocadotea.com.

BELLA VADO. Corrine da Silva and her husband run this small family-owned business in Valley Center. Bella Vado makes avocado oil as well as avocado-oil products like soap and hand cream, all from local avocados. www.bellavado.com.

THE SPOILED AVOCADO. Located in downtown Fallbrook, this shop offers avocado-themed fashion, food, toys and more. 116 North Main Avenue, Fallbrook, CA; (760) 451-6445.

SUGGESTED READING

Burningham, John. *Avocado Baby*. London: Red Fox Picture Books, 1994.

Dike, Colette. *The Ultimate Avocado Cookbook: 50 Modern, Stylish & Delicious Recipes to Feed Your Avocado Addiction*. New York: Skyhorse Publishing, 2019.

Ferroni, Lara. *An Avocado a Day*. Seattle, WA: Sasquatch Books, 2017.

Miller, Jeff. *Avocado: A Global History*. London: Reaktion Books, 2020.

WHERE TO FIND CALIFORNIA AVOCADOS

Different varieties of California avocados are available throughout the year at hundreds of small fruit stands, nurseries and farmers' markets from Morro Bay to Chula Vista. The state's official avocado season, however, runs from spring through summer or early fall. You can find California avocados in larger markets in the western region of the United States during this time. According to CAC, the following stores regularly offer California avocados in season: Albertsons, Bristol Farms, Costco, Gelson's Markets, Kroger, Mollie Stones, Raley's, Safeway, Sam's Club, Sprouts, Stater Bros., Walmart, Whole Foods and others. Look for the California label.

There are several small companies that sell California avocados as part of a regular "avocado of the month" program. Longtime growers Ralph and Peggy Foster offer such a service through their site at www.avocadomonthly. com. Another online store is Escondido grower Ben Holtz's www. californiaavocadosdirect.com. Find more online and through social media.

PURCHASING AN AVOCADO TREE

Dozens of retailers in California carry potted avocado trees for sale, which they acquire from large wholesale nurseries like Brokaw Nursery, Everde Growers, Maddock Ranch Nursery and Durling Nursery. There are many options for backyard growers when it comes to buying a tree, whether it is Hass or one of the more unusual (but delicious) varieties such as GEM, Fuerte or Reed. Lowe's, Home Depot and Armstrong Garden Center offer high-quality trees at reasonable prices. For expert advice and better selection, consider purchasing from a small family-owned nursery.

....

El Pollo Loco Avocado Salsa (Almost!)
Courtesy of El Pollo Loco's Culinary Team, 2024

I have always been a fan of El Pollo Loco's delicious avocado salsa, which it makes from more than 13 million avocados every year. Fl Pollo Loco has allowed us to share the following recipe. It is nearly identical to the one it makes fresh daily at its five hundred locations across the United States.

INGREDIENTS
1 medium avocado
2 serrano chilies (halved and stems removed)
2 cups fresh cilantro (chopped and stems removed)
2 limes, juiced
3 teaspoons garlic powder
1 teaspoon onion powder
2 teaspoons kosher salt
2½ cups cold water
¾ cup white onion, diced small (about ½ an onion)

Cut the avocado in half, remove the pit and scoop the flesh into a blender. Add the serrano chilies, cilantro, lime juice, garlic powder, onion powder, salt and water with the avocado and then blend everything on medium-high speed for 10 to 20 seconds until well combined and no big pieces of cilantro are visible. If your avocado is large, add up to ½ cup more cold water to thin out the salsa. Pour the contents of the blender into a medium mixing bowl, add in the diced onion and mix with a spoon until evenly dispersed. Transfer the salsa to an airtight container and chill in the refrigerator for 15 minutes before eating. Makes 1 quart.

BIBLIOGRAPHY

All web sources were accessed in 2023 or 2024. The California Avocado Society yearbook is hereafter marked as "CAS."

General Sources

Alder, Greg. *Yard Posts*. Blog. https://gregalder.com/yardposts.
Arpaia, Mary Lu, Eric Focht, et al. UC–Riverside Avocado Variety Collection. https://avocado.ucr.edu.
Avocado Society. https://californiaavocadosociety.org.
Avocadosource. The Hofshi Foundation. https://www.avocadosource.com.
Bender, Gary. *Avocado Production in California: A Cultural Handbook for Growers*. 2nd ed. Joint Publication of University of California Cooperative Extension and CAS, 2015.
California Avocado Commission. https://californiaavocadogrowers.com.
Hass Avocado Board. https://hassavocadoboard.com.
Kerr, William Sterling, III. "The Avocado Industry in Southern California: A Study of Location, Perception, and Prospect." PhD diss., University of Oklahoma, 1970.
Linden, Tim, ed. *From the Grove*. California Avocado Commission, 2011–.
Shepherd, Jack, and Gary S. Bender. "A History of the Avocado Industry in California." CAS 85 (2001): 29–50.

Avocados Before California

Arpaia, Mary Lu, Eric Focht, et al. UC–Riverside Avocado Variety Collection. https://avocado.ucr.edu.

CAS 81. "The Most Important Known Reference to the Avocado in Literature, Down to the End of the Seventeenth Century" (1997): 172–74.

Funnell, Rachael. "Fact Check: Are Avocados Really Named After Testicles?" IFL Science, September 6, 2022. www.iflscience.com.

Galindo-Tovar, María Elena, Amaury M. Arzate-Fernández, Nisao Ogata-Aguilar and Ivonne Landero-Torres. "The Avocado (Persea Americana, Lauraceae) Crop in Mesoamerica: 10,000 Years of History." *Harvard Papers in Botany* 12 (December 2007): 325–34.

McPherson, William. "Early Account of the Avocados in America." CAS 39 (1955): 87–88.

Miller, Jeff. *Avocado: A Global History*. London: Reaktion Books, 2020.

Popenoe, Wilson. "Early History of the Avocado." CAS 47 (1963): 19–24.

Popenoe, Wilson, et al. "The Avocado Has Many Names." CAS 81 (1997): 155–62.

Schroeder, C.A. "Dampier's Early Account of the Avocado." CAS 63 (1979): 77–78.

———. "Some Useful Plants of the Botanical Family Lauraceae." CAS 59 (1975–76): 30–34.

Smith, K. Annabelle. "Why the Avocado Should Have Gone the Way of the Dodo." *Smithsonian Magazine* (October 24, 2013).

Spilde, Ingrid. "Why Does the Avocado Have Such Huge Seeds?" November 20, 2020. ScienceNorway.com.

Storey, W.B. "What Kind of Fruit Is the Avocado?" CAS 57 (1973–74): 70–71.

Storey, W.B., Bob Bergh and G.A. Zentmyer. "The Origin, Indigenous Range, and Dissemination of the Avocado." CAS 70 (1986): 127–33.

Coming to America

Bertelli, Brad. "The Avocado's Arrival to North America and the Island Chain." *Keys Weekly*, October 16, 2023. keysweekly.com.

———. "The Story of Dr. Henry Perrine." *Keys Weekly*, March 15, 2021. keysweekly.com.

Coit, John Eliot. "The Importance of the Fuerte Variety." CAS 52 (1968): 35–37.

Condit, Ira J. "History of the Avocado and Its Varieties in California with a Check List of All Named Varieties." CAS 2 (1916): 105–44.

DanielRC2014. "In 1913, Southern California Was Under the Polar Vortex. It Transformed the Region's Economy, Helped Found a UC Campus and Gave Rise to a U.S. President." May 10, 2021. Exploresoutherncal.wordpress.com.

Edible South Florida. "The Case for Florida Avocados." September 6, 2020. EdibleSouthFlorida.com.

Geisseler, Daniel, and William R. Horwath. "Citrus Production in California." *University of California–Davis Publications* (2016): 1–3.

Handwerk, Brian. "Holy Guacamole: How the Hass Avocado Conquered the World." *Smithsonian Magazine* (July 28, 2017). Smithsonianmag.com.

Hodgson, Robert W. *The California Avocado Industry*. Berkeley: University of California, College of Agriculture Publications, 1930.

Knight, Robert J., Jr., and Carl W. Campbell. "Ecological Adaptation and the Evolution of Modern Avocado Cultivars." *Tropical Research & Education Center, University of Florida* 1, no. 3 (2004).

Olmstead, Alan L., and Paul W. Rhode. *A History of California Agriculture*. Davis: University of California Agriculture and Natural Resources Publications, 2017.

Pacific Rural Press 35, no. 15. "The Nursery Business" (April 14, 1888).

Palmer, Sarah R.W. "Henry Perrine, Pioneer Botanist and Horticulturist." *Florida Historical Society Quarterly* 5, no. 2 (October 1926): 112–15.

Poole, Dwight, and Mildred Poole. "From Pigs to Riches." CAS 51 (1967): 25–28.

Popenoe, Wilson. "The Development of the Avocado Industry." *Pomona College Journal of Economic Botany* (1911).

———. "The Parent Fuerte Tree at Atlixco, Mexico." CAS 10 (1925–26): 24–34.

Reid, Eliza P. *Historical and Literary Botany: Containing the Qualities, Anecdotes, and Superstitions, Relative to Trees, Plants, and Flowers, Which Are Mentioned in Sacred and Profane History*. London, 1826.

Birth of an Industry

Beach, John B. "The Avocado in Florida." CAS 2 (1916): 165–68.

CAS 1. "The California Avocado Association Is Issuing in Folder Form the Following Suggestions for Preparing the Avocado for the Table" (1915): 91–93.

CAS 59. "Wilson Popenoe…Vaya con Dios" (1975–76): 10.

Coit, J. Eliot. "Avocado Culture: A New Horticultural Industry." CAS 13 (1928): 91 93.

Coolidge, D.W. "Seven Truths About the Avocado." CAS 7 (1920–21): 19–21.

Fulfer, Johnny. "Free Trade vs. Protectionism: The Tariff Debate in the United States." *Economic History* blog, May 23, 2021. economic-historian.com.

Gómez-López, Vicente M. "Fruit Characterization of High Oil Content Avocado Varieties." *Scientia Agricola* 59, no. 2 (April–June 2002): 403–6.

Hart, Edwin G. "The Association and Its Purposes." CAS 1 (1915): 7–9.

Hodgson, Robert W. "The Florida Avocado Industry—a Survey." CAS 10 (1925–26): 60–71.

King, Dana C. "Marketing Obstacles and Problems." CAS 2 (1916): 32–37.

Liebhold, Andrew M., and Robert L. Griffin. "The Legacy of Charles Marlatt and Efforts to Limit Plant Pest Invasions." *American Entomologist* 62, no. 4 (Winter 2016): 218–27.

McFarland, J. Horace. "Plant Quarantine: A Footnote to the Discussion." *Atlantic Monthly* (August 1925): 241–45.

Notice of Quarantine No. 12: Avocado Seed Quarantine. USDA under B.T. Galloway, February 27, 1914.

Popenoe, F.O. "Varieties of the Avocado." CAS 1 (1915): 44–69.

Popenoe, F.O., and Wilson Popenoe. "Avocado Value and Propagation." *Pacific Rural Press* 89 (January 23, 1915): 108–9.

Popenoe, Wilson. "The Avocado in Florida and Other Lands." CAS 1 (1915): 29–42.

———. "Hunting Avocados." CAS 17 (1932): 180–82.

Rock, Robert C., and Robert G. Platt. "Economic Trends in the California Avocado Industry." CAS 57 (1973–74): 46–56.

Shepherd, Jack. "The Most Important Thing." CAS 61 (1977): 10–16.

———. "Recognition of the 75th Anniversary: Commemoration and Commitment." CAS 74 (1990): 151–57.

———. "The Views of Janus." CAS 48 (1964): 22–29.

Spitzzeri, Paul R. "'The Hanging Gardens of Southern California': Edwin G. Hart and the Avocado Subdivisions of Hacienda Heights and La Habra Heights, 1913–1930." *Homestead*, a publication of the Homestead Museum, June 28, 2020.

Stonebrook, H.B. "Discussion of the Florida Avocado Situation." CAS 10 (1925–26): 71–72.

Wolff, K.L. "Enforcing the Avocado Standardization Act." CAS 10 (1925–26): 77–81.

Marketing the Aristocrat of Salad Fruits

Alger, Eulalia B. "Avocado Recipes." CAS 20 (1935): 113–15.

Andrews, Richard. "Calavo: Growth and Progress of the Avocado Cooperative." *Magazine of the Pacific*, December 1937.

Barrett, Carter. "The Pilgrimage to Atlixco." CAS 23 (1938): 42–48.

Calavo News. "University Reports on By-Product Research." June 22, 1927.

CAS 23. "Report of the Variety Committee." (1938): 28–35.

CAS 60. "Dr. J. Eliot Coit (1880–1976)." (1976): 11–13.

Coit, J. Eliot. "Avocado Varieties." CAS 41 (1957): 37–42.

Crosby, Leigh. "Calavo Advertising." CAS 14 (1929): 68–75.

Cruess, W.V., and S.K. Mitra. "Avocado By-Products." CAS 2 (1916): 16–19.

Debard, A.S. "Avocado Tree Decline." CAS 28 (1943): 39–40.

Hirtzler, Victor. "The Avocado for the Table." CAS (1917–18): 51–53.

Hodgkin, George B. "Calavo." CAS 11 (1925–26): 42–44.

Keller, Lester. "How Far Can We Go with the Avocado as a Food? Will People Eat It, and to What Extent?" CAS 4 (1918–19): 26–29.

Kerr, William Sterling, III. "The Avocado Industry in Southern California: A Study of Location, Perception, and Prospect." PhD diss., University of Oklahoma, 1970.

Le Blanc, Alejandro. "Message from Señor Alejandro Le Blanc." CAS 23 (1938): 37–38.

Ryerson, Knowles A., et al. *Avocado Culture in California*. Berkeley: University of California, 1928.

Shamel, A.D. "Avocado Studies in Mexico in 1938." CAS 23 (1938): 67–85.

Shepherd, Jack. "The Ever-Whirling Wheel of Change…Or Time Turned Topsy-Turvy." CAS 72 (1988): 159–63.

———. "The Most Important Thing." CAS 61 (1977): 10–16.

Shepherd, Jack, and Gary S. Bender. "A History of the Avocado Industry in California." CAS 85 (2001): 29–50.

Whitney, Guy. "California Avocado Industry." CAS 88 (2005): 47–53.

Young, Floyd D. "Lessons from the 1937 Freeze." CAS 21 (1937): 90–93.

The Commercial Era Begins

California Avocado Commission. 2021 Statewide Avocado Acreage & Condition Analysis. Prepared by Land IQ, October 2021.

CAS 48. "John Eliot Coit: 'The Father of the Avocado Industry.'" (1964): 19–20.

Collins, G.N. *The Avocado: A Salad Fruit from the Tropics*. Vol. 77. Washington, D.C.: USDA, Bureau of Plant Industry, 1905.

Eidermiller, D.I. "Economic Geography of Avocado Growing in San Diego County." PhD diss. University of California, 1951.

Gustafson, C.D. "San Diego County Avocado Industry." CAS 42 (1958): 58–60.

Hass, Rudolph G. "Avocado (U.S. Patent No. 16,837)." U.S. Patent and Trademark Office, 1935. https://www.avocadosource.com/links/HassPatent_1935.pdf.

Kerr, William Sterling, III. "The Avocado Industry in Southern California: A Study of Location, Perception, and Prospect." PhD diss., University of Oklahoma, 1970.

Pehrson, J.E. "Urbanization and Avocado Growing." CAS 46 (1962): 46–48.

Pendleton, J.H. "Notes." CAS 4 (1918–19): 86.

Popenoe, F.O. "San Diego County Avocado History." CAS 12 (1927): 41–48.

Rock, Robert C., and Robert G. Platt. "Economic Trends in the California Avocado Industry." CAS 52 (1968): 61–80.

Shepherd, Jack. "Avocado Marketing." CAS 30 (1946): 123–26.

———. "Market Acceptance of New Varieties." CAS 34 (1949): 118–22.

————. "One Strong from Many Weak." CAS 46 (1962): 29–32.

Stephens, Thomas S., et al. "Preparation of a Frozen Avocado Mixture for Guacamole." *Rio Grande Valley Horticultural Society* 11 (1957): 82–89.

Todd, Ted. "The Avocado Variety Situation Today." CAS 50 (1966): 21–25.

Tropical Fruits for California. Marketing brochure. West India Gardens, April 1, 1913.

Avocados Go Mainstream

Berger, Kay. "Avocado Marketing Problem." CAS 56 (1972): 28–30.

Bergh, Bob. "Industry Funding of Avocado Research." CAS 70 (1986): 71–78.

Brokaw, Hank. "In Memoriam, Dr. George Zentmyer." CAS 86 (2002): 46–48.

California Avocado Advisory Board. "California Avocado Acreage by Counties." CAS 51 (1967): 70.

Carman, Hoy F., and R. Kim Craft. *An Economic Evaluation of California Avocado Industry Marketing Programs (1961–1995)*. Giannini Foundation Research Report, No. 345, April 1998.

Flores, Antonio. "How the U.S. Hispanic Population Is Changing." Pew Research Center, September 18, 2017.

Freistadt, David. "An Appraisal of Gwen and Whitsell." CAS 69 (1985): 29–30.

Fulton, Dave. "50-Year Calavo Push Makes Avocados Famous." *The Packer*, February 2, 1974, 2A.

Gustafson, C.D. "The Avocado Industry in San Diego County." CAS 61 (1977): 44–47.

Kerr, William Sterling, III. "The Avocado Industry in Southern California: A Study of Location, Perception, and Prospect." PhD diss., University of Oklahoma, 1970.

Linden, Tim. "Camlam Farms: Deep, Deep Roots and a Promising Future." *From the Grove* (Spring 2023): 18–20.

Pinkerton, Ralph M. "Avocado Advertising Is a Profitable Investment." CAS 47 (1963): 26–27.

————. "Marketing the 1982–1983 California Avocado Crop." CAS 66 (1982): 45–48.

Rivard, Ry. "The Tax Loophole that Gave Rise to San Diego's Avocado Boom." *Voice of San Diego*, May 26, 2016. voiceofsandiego.org.

Rock, Robert C. "Expansion in the California Avocado Industry." CAS 57 (1973–74): 25–31.

Shepherd, Jack. "Even a Better Mousetrap Needs Advertising." CAS 28 (1964): 51–55.

————. "The Ever-Whirling Wheel of Change…Or Time Turned Topsy-Turvy." CAS 72 (1988): 159–63.

Todd, Ted. "The Avocado Variety Situation Today." CAS 50 (1966): 21–25.

Avocado Land Becomes Avocado World

Affleck, Mark. "The International Avocado Industry: A Global Perspective." CAS 70 (1986): 51–55.

———. "World Avocado Market: A Brief Review." *Proc. of Second World Avocado Congress* (1992): 621–24.

Ambuul, Chris. "An Afternoon with Mike Sanders and Bob Lucy." CAS 96 (2013): 41–53.

Bartash, Jeffry. "Ole! Mexico Becomes Biggest U.S. Importer Amid Tensions with China." *Marketwatch* 29 (November 7, 2023). www.marketwatch.com.

Bellamore, Tom. "Mexican Avocados: History…The Full Story." CAS 86 (2002): 51–71.

Calavo Growers Inc. https://calavo.com.

CAS 19. "Avocado Planting in Russia" (1934): 115.

CAS 30. "Wilson Popenoe Receives Society Award of Honor" (1946): 99.

Chapman, Robert. "Picking and Boxing Calavos for the Packing House." CAS 16 (1931): 115.

Chawkins, Steve. "Gil Henry Dies at 88; Revolutionized Avocado Industry." *Los Angeles Times*, June 3, 2013.

Christie, A.W. "The Aims and Accomplishments of the California Avocado Society." CAS 33 (1948): 135–36.

Christie, Arthur W. "Some Fundamentals of Picking, Packing, and Marketing." CAS 30 (1945): 55–56.

Colin, Salvador Sanchez. "The Importance of the California Avocado Society—An Appraisal from Mexico." CAS 72 (1988): 89–96.

Crane, Avi. "Industry Structure and the Marketing of California Avocados." *Proc. of Third World Avocado Congress* (1995): 445–50.

———. "North American Free Trade Agreement." CAS 76 (1992): 145–50.

———. "Technical and Economic Aspects of the Harvesting, Packing, and Transporting of Avocados in the United States of America." CAS 80 (1996): 45–55.

Francis, H. Leonard. "Mexico—Is It Really What We Hear? CAS 77 (1993): 59–65.

Freistadt, David. "The Handlers' Contribution." CAS 52 (1968): 52–54.

Fresh Plaza. "Looking Inside the Packing House of a California Avocado Grower-Shipper." July 17, 2018. freshplaza.com.

Glorioso, Jennifer, and Mitchell Comstock. *Andy the Avocado Goes from the Field to Your Fork*. Oxnard, CA: Mission Produce, 2016.

Gustafson, C.D. "Avocado Growers' Study Mission #2 to Mexico—1970." CAS 55 (1971–72): 61–67.

———. "1976 World Avocado Production." CAS 60 (1976): 74–90.

———. "The Summary of Our Trip to Mexico." CAS 52 (1968): 173–76.

Hass Avocado Board. *Avocado Quality Manual: A Guide to Best Practices*. Irvine, CA, 2020.

Henry Avocado. www.henryavocado.com.

Henry, Charles Oilman. "How to Benefit from 'Pre-Ripe.'" CAS 68 (1984): 37–41.

Henry, Warren. "The Role of the Independent Packer in the Avocado Industry." CAS 46 (1962): 27–28.

Hodgkin, George B. "Handling Methods." CAS 10 (1924–25): 67–68.

———. "A Pilgrimage (1929) to the Parent Fuerte Tree." CAS 64 (1980): 63–66.

Huvard, Richard, and Liz Wheaton. *I Am an Avocado*. Santa Paula, CA: Calavo Growers Inc., 2004.

Index Fresh. www.indexfresh.com.

Kerr, William Sterling, III. "The Avocado Industry in Southern California: A Study of Location, Perception, and Prospect." PhD diss., University of Oklahoma, 1970.

Krishna, Mrinalini. "How Much Does the U.S. Import from Mexico?" Investopedia, April 2, 2023. https://www.investopedia.com.

McCormac, James. "The California Avocado Society." *From the Grove* (Summer 2012): 40–42.

Mission Produce. www.missionproduce.com.

Newman, C.V. "Pilgrimage to the Original Fuerte Tree." CAS 15 (1930): 113–17.

Paz-Vega, Ramon. "Mexican Avocados: Threat or Opportunity for California?" CAS 73 (1989): 87–106.

Preston, T.E. Lynn. "CADO—The Avocado Handlers Association." CAS 46 (1962): 23–25.

Produce News. "Avocado Pioneer Victor Tokar Dies." December 13, 2013.

———. "Eco Farms Celebrates 50 Years of Avocados." June 22, 2022. https://theproducenews.com.

Shaulis, Robert. "West Pak Story: Carrying a Legacy Forward." *The Snack* 29. www.thesnack.net.

Shepherd, Jack. "The Most Important Thing." CAS 61 (1977): 10–16.

Spezzano, Richard. "Growers/Packer/Retailers—Partners in Progress." CAS 70 (1986): 63–67.

Tokar, Victor. "The History of Commercial Avocado Ripening." CAS 90 (2007).

Vision Fruitcola. "Interview with Steve Barnard, Founder and CEO of Mission Produce" (July 2021).

Woodger, Elizabeth R. "Wilson Popenoe, American Horticulturist, Educator, and Explorer." *Huntia* 5, no. 1 (1983): 17–22.

The Avocado Revolution

Affleck, Mark. "In Memoriam: So Long, Ralph Pinkerton." CAS 87 (2004–5): 27–28.

Associated Press. "U.S. Suspends Mexican Avocado Imports After Threat to Inspector." February 13, 2022.

Avocados from Mexico. "Avocado Industry Welcomes Jalisco to U.S. Mexican Avocado Imports" (December 16, 2021).

Bastida, Olmo. "Current Situation of the Fresh Avocado Market in the U.S." ProducePay, October 5, 2023. www.producepay.com.

Bauer, Ella E., and Nikki Ford. "Avocado Health Benefits from A to Z." CAS (Q3 2022).

Bergh, Bob. "Nutritious Value of Avocado." CAS 76 (1992): 123–35.

California Avocado Commission. Industry Statistical Data (1971–2022). www.californiaavocadogrowers.com.

———. 2022 California Avocado Acreage Report. Prepared by Land IQ, September 2022.

CAS 17. "Myer Edward Jaffa—An Appreciation" (1932): 187–88.

CAS 27. "Army-Navy Avocado Business Increasing (Reprint from 1943 *Calavo News*)" (1943): 75–76.

Climate Rights International. "U.S./Mexico: U.S. Senators Urge Action on Mexican Avocados." February 8, 2024.

Escobedo, Emiliano. "If Past Is Prologue, Get Ready for a New Wave of Avocado Category Success." CAS 95 (2012): 91–101.

Ford, Nikki A. "Avocados Are Heart-Healthy." CAS (Q2 2020): 23–25.

Francis, Len. "An Appreciation of Jack Shepherd." CAS 82 (1998): 27–28.

From the Grove. "FDA Update: Avocados Now Considered 'Healthy.'" (Winter 2016): 20–21.

Grant, Wilson C. "Influence of Avocados on Serum Cholesterol." CAS 44 (1960): 79–88.

Gray, Louise. *Avocado Anxiety: And Other Stories About Where Your Food Comes From.* New York: Bloomsbury Publishing, 2023.

Imbert, Eric. "World Avocado Market Projection Up to the Year 2030, Version 2.0." *FruiTrop* (May–June 2023).

Kennedy, Lucy, director. *Rotten.* "The Avocado War." Season 2, Episode 1. Aired October 4, 2019. Netflix.

Linden, Tim. "European Avocado Market Continues to Expand." *From the Grove* (Fall 2021): 14–16.

———. "HAB Continues to Represent the Entire Industry." *From the Grove* (Spring 2013): 41.

———. "HAB Poised for Future Growth." *From the Grove* (Spring 2012): 34.

———. "Health Claim for Avocados Approved." *From the Grove* (Spring 2017): 36–38.

McDonald, Jeff. "San Diego County Water Board Accepts $25 Million to Settle Lawsuit Over Fallbrook, Rainbow Departure." *San Diego Union-Tribune*, December 22, 2023.

Moslimani, Mohamad, et al. "Fact Sheet: Facts on Hispanics of Mexican Origin in the U.S., 2021." Pew Research Center, August 16, 2023.

Nguyen, Alexander. "County Leaders Rally Against Water 'Divorce' with Fallbrook and Rainbow." KPBS, July 23, 2023. KPBS.org.

Obregon, Jose Luis. "Hass Avocado Marketers Gain Strength, Retain Independence." CAS 93 (2010): 75–83.

Pinkerton, Ralph M., et al. "The California Avocado Commission—A Profile." CAS 65 (1981): 93–100.

Produce News. "CAC's Nutrition Advisory Committee Chairman Retires." December 12, 2005.

Romero, Simon, and Emiliano Rodriguez Mega. "Americans Love Avocados. It's Killing Mexico's Forests." *New York Times*, November 28, 2022.

Smith, Joshua Emerson. "Why the Cost of Water in San Diego Has Blown Past L.A." Associated Press, February 13, 2022.

Wolk, Charley. "California Avocados: Competing, and Winning: The White-Hot Marketing Game." *Proc. of World Avocado Congress* 5 (2003): 797–802.